CW01662881

Yorkshire Maps and Map-Makers

£1.75

Yorkshire Maps and Map-Makers

by

Arthur Raistrick,
M.Sc., Ph.D., D. Litt.

Dalesman Books
1979

The Dalesman Publishing Company Ltd.,
Clapham (via Lancaster), North Yorkshire

First published 1969
Reprinted 1979

ISBN: 0 85206 011 4

The cover picture:
Part of a map by Speed, 1610, based upon Saxton's earlier map, but embellished and improved.

Printed in Great Britain by Galava Printing Co. Ltd.,
Hallam Road, Nelson, Lancashire

Contents

Illustrations

An Introduction

MAPS are an invention of comparatively recent centuries. The question naturally arises: "How did people find their way about the country in the early days before maps and guide-books were made?" One remembers Mark Twain's comment in his book *Yankee at the Court of King Arthur*, when the Boss set out with his lady to deliver her captive friends, and naturally asked the way to the place of their captivity. She told him that the way wound so much, first this way, then that, that it was beyond the wit of man to say how it went or which was its direction. They just blundered on in faith, and sooner or later—and generally much later—stumbled upon a remembered landmark and eventually arrived. Was such haphazard progression characteristic of those early days, or were there known paths and ways to help a traveller?

There is a steady accumulation of evidence that as far back as the Middle Stone Age, men were making their ways, season after season, over the same ridges of high ground along the upper edges of the forests from Denmark across the swamps which then filled the southern end of what is now the North Sea basin, on to the chalk and jurassic ridges of East Anglia and Lincolnshire, and so on to the Pennines. The distribution of their remains strongly suggests that they travelled regularly along some of our Pennine Dales' "edges" round about the 1,000 to 1,500 feet level, and started tracks which grew in use and importance with the passing of later centuries. Many a hillside track parallel with the run of the valley originated in this or in later pre-historic periods, and the knowledge of them was, no doubt, a valued and well-cherished possession of some of these people.

The tracks from the East Coast and from the head of the Humber across the Vale of York by the morainic gravel ridges of York and Escrick; over the gravels of lower Wharfedale on to the ridge of Rombalds Moor; further west along the high ground between Colne and Burnley and so to the Ribble estuary, were well-known and in constant use during the Bronze Age and to describe adequately the abundant prehistoric tracks would need a book to itself. We shall have to leave them with this scanty mention and pass on to the first organised system of roads in a period of directed travel—that of the Roman occupation.

Part of the Roman plan of campaign, and indeed, an essential part, was the construction of a complete system of military and post roads over the whole country, and the necessary work was carried out mainly during the first century of our era. In Yorkshire we have many sections of this road system, the North Road through Doncaster, Tadcaster, Boroughbridge, Catterick and eventually to the Roman Wall in Northumberland; cross roads from Boroughbridge to Manchester via Ilkley, from Chester to York by the mid-Pennines, from Ribchester over Bowland to Carlisle, and so on, too many to enumerate here. How were these roads used, and were there any guides to them, or maps of them, or were they signposted? These are legitimate questions that naturally spring to the minds of modern road users.

It is certain that the military commanders in the various Roman forts, and particularly at the greater cities like York and Chester, had a key to the road system and could direct their troops or messengers how to get to any desired place. In the early third century official documentary guides were prepared, the one for this country being the *Itinerarium Antonini*—a list of the military stations along the principal roads, with their distances one from another, given in Roman miles, which were nearly equal to our present mile. Along many of the roads, mileposts were erected and some of these survive to the present day. The milestones were not necessarily placed to indicate mileage, but often merely commemorated the maker of the road, though they were placed at regular intervals. At least eight have been found in Yorkshire, mainly near Castleton, Aldborough, and on Stainmore. Two were found in 1926 while ditching on the north side of the Roman road over Stainmore leading from Bowes (*Lavatrae*) to Brough (*Verterae*).

Each is a squat cylindrical pillar of gritstone with an inscription cut on it in the usual Roman script using many abbreviations. These milestones can now be seen in the County Hall, Northallerton. One is dedicated to or commemorates the Emperor Probus, 276-282 A.D., and the other Carus, 282-283 A.D., the inscription on one is:-

IMPCM
AVRELIO
PROBO
PFAVG

Translated it reads: "To the Emperor Caesar Marcus Aurelius Probus, pious, fortunate and august." Some of the milestones have a distance on them, but this is by no means a general practice.

The commander of a garrison, with his copy of the itinerary, could instruct and despatch soldiers by the most direct way, giving them a copy of the relevant part of the guide, and could also communicate by a system of organised "post" messengers with other parts and cities. Some of the post-ways were by no means direct, but were probably established according to the particular location of troops, or by some custom so that, for instance, at one time a post message from Ribchester to Carlisle went by way of Ilkley, Boroughbridge, and Stainmore —and not by the direct route up Lunedale.

We know from discoveries on the continent that in the third century there were a few copies of the itineraries in private civilian hands, and that some of these were accompanied by approximate maps. A wealthy person wishing to travel on private business could obtain such at a price. It would be possible for citizens in the civilian settlements attached to most of the larger forts and cities to learn the facts of the itinerary and so know which road to take and how far to go to get from one place to another.

Besides the Roman roads there were many older, native tracks, knowledge of which was probably a jealously guarded secret among the Brigantes, tracks by which native intercourse was maintained and movement made across the network of "policed" Roman roads.

For many centuries after the withdrawal of the Romans their roads remained the principal lines of movement for long-distance travel, and in the lowlands certainly exercised a great influence in determining the pattern of Anglian and Danish settlement. Actually there was very little in the way of travel until the late Middle Ages, when the monasteries, with their widespread estates, made great use of roads between the parent monasteries and their many outlying manors and granges. Many of these roads were marked by wayside crosses, but nothing in the way of signpost or map was made. Roads beyond the village were little used except by officials of the monasteries, manor courts, or castles, and these users were well instructed in the way.

Any other traveller would have to ask his way by stages—he could learn from one monastery or castle the way to the next or possibly be directed from one village to another, though it meant a more tedious progression. A few traders and chapmen travelled from the great fairs to the country villages and small towns and so gradually established a network of market roads. The preaching friars seem to have wandered everywhere.

Bridges were few and far between and fords were often treacherous. The maintenance of bridges, the provision of ferries across rivers, or the guidance of travellers through forests or across bad ground were favourite works of religious charity and were often endowed as a mark of piety by wealthy persons. Between the fixed points of bridges and fords, ways were doubtful and tracks were rough and changeable, often passing through dangerous forest or across wild moorland where outlaws of the Robin Hood type were by no means mere characters of fiction or legend. The wise traveller usually attached himself to a company of fellow travellers big enough to employ a guide and to afford protection from the dangers of the road.

The vast importance of bridges as fixed points in the routes is evident in all mediaeval literature and legend, and some bridges were put in the care of hermits or chantry priests, or like the Wakefield and Rotherham bridges, had chantry chapels built on the bridge itself. The importance of bridges is also seen when one reads the journeys of Leland.

John Leland was authorised in 1533, to visit monasteries, chapels, colleges, and all libraries or places where there might be material for a history of England, and to take extracts and make copies. In 1539 he started on a journey through England to view the land he was writing about, and after six years' almost continuous travel, wrote his *Itinerary* and brought together many notes on the country as he saw it. Much of his journal concerns the libraries, castles, and antiquities which he saw, but it also mentions in great detail his routes, and here the bridges and fords dominate the account.

"From York to Kexby Bridge by Champaine (cultivated country) meately fertile a v. Miles. This Bridge of 3. fair Arches of Stone standith on the praty Ryver of Darwent, that commith by Malton, and as I gesse this Bridge is towards the Midle way bytwixt Malton and Wreshil, wher about Darwent goith ynto Ouse."

His next comment, for the information of travellers is "Bridges upon Darwent above Kexby, Staneford Bridge a 2. Miles of. Buttercrambridge a miles. Ousehambridge a 2 miles of. Kirkham a 2 Miles or more . . . " and so on to the head of the river. For each river he gives similar information but sometimes in a little more detail, as in Nidderdale:-

"Nid ryver risethe muche by West 5 Miles above Pateley Bridge of Wood . . . From Pateley Bridge and Village to Newbridge of Tymber 3 Miles. Thens to Killinghal Bridge of one greate Arche of Stone 3 Miles and 3 Miles to Gnaresbrughe, where first is the West Bridge of 3 Arches of Stone, and then a little lower Marche Bridge of 3 Arches. Both these bridges serve the town of Knaresborow . . . "

Near Wetherby he was impressed by the goodness of the Roman road, still in use, and says, "Thens over a stone Bridge on Warfe to . . . on Watheling Streate a 6 Miles, and or ever I cam to this thoroughfare I saw by the space of 2 or 3 Miles the very playn Crest of Watheling Streat. Thens by the strait Crest of Watheling Streat a 3 Miles or more and then leving it on the right Hond I went to Brotherton a 3 Miles: and then by a causey of Stone with divers bridges over it to dreane the low Medow Waters on the lift Hand into Aire Ryver about a Mile to Fery-Bridge . . . ."

Between the various bridges and fords, Leland comments often that the way lay over rough "moorish" ground, or across wild stony wastes, and in many parts it is evident that he took a general line only from one point to the other. He asked his way about the country, being a generation too soon to have the advantage of the first county maps, made by our fellow Yorkshireman, Saxton, in 1577.

From other sources and travels we know that over much of the country, ways from one part to another were known only to local people and to few of them, and that a general progression was made by hiring guides for comparatively short distances, unless the way lay along one of the old Roman roads or on a well-used way between two market towns of importance. Leland's directions, "west a 3 Miles," and so on, are as precise as any that are available in his time, and a journey must have been largely a venture of faith, with little knowledge of the kind of way or the length of time it was going to take. Nearly all journeying was by horseback, there were few wagons and very few roads on which they could pass, and goods were still moved by pack-horses, mainly traversing the higher fell-side roads and greenways, keeping well above the swampy valley bottoms, and descending only to the bridges and fords.

Early Map-Makers

FEW country-lovers today could imagine setting out to visit a new piece of country without equipping themselves with a map of the area, poring over it in advance to learn the features of the countryside, taking it with them as a trusty companion and guide, and then on many later occasions bringing it out to refresh memories and to re-live the happy days spent with it in the field. The map is such a normal part of outdoor life today that perhaps we take it too much for granted and give very little thought to its history and to the work that has gone into the making of the many maps we possess.

The map as we buy it today is a comparatively modern production, scarcely a hundred years old, though its progenitors have a history reaching back over two centuries earlier. We might well be moved to ask, "Who were the early map makers, what kind of men were they, how did they work and what were their maps like?" Some of the earliest maps adorn our walls as decorative pictures, gay in their colouring (though this is not always original) and made attractive by numerous coats of arms and by the ships or monsters that lighten the duller expanse of the sea; sometimes there are decorative borders, or an interesting plan of some ancient city. Some attempt must be made to answer these questions before the extraordinary work of the Ordnance Survey and the maps they have produced is discussed.

Until the sixteenth century we can say that maps were practically non-existent in this country. About the middle of that century, maps of Great Britain or of England and Wales were made but these were mainly based upon the ancient geography of Ptolemy. With advances in the art of engraving, a school of map engravers and printers developed in Holland, producing large atlases of the known world, with maps of Britain on a moderately large scale such as Mercator's map (1564) with a scale of about 14 miles to one inch included in them. We owe the idea and practice of producing larger scale maps of the individual counties within a country to a Yorkshireman, Christopher Saxton, and for more than 250 years this custom of treating the counties as the unit in map-making has persisted.

Very little is known of the early life of Saxton, except that he was born in the West Riding, possibly at Dunningley, near Wakefield, and in the year 1542 or 1544. The slight evidence available favours the earlier date, 1542. The family of Saxton was living in Dunningley, in the parish of West Ardsley, all the latter half of the sixteenth century and Christopher lived there and was buried at West Ardsley. Although Dunningley is only a small cluster of houses (near West Ardsley Collieries) still it is marked on Saxton's map of Yorkshire, 1577, and more surprising it is included on his general map of England and Wales, 1584. The date of his death is not known as the church at West Ardsley has been rebuilt and any tombstone or memorial to him that may have been there has been lost. The parish registers for the early seventeenth century are very incomplete. Sir G. Fordham, however, by an exhaustive examination of documents of many kinds has demonstrated that Saxton was still alive in 1610 and that he might have died before 1616.

Christopher Saxton was employed as servant to Thomas Seckford who was Master of the Requests at the court of Queen Elizabeth, and a man of considerable influence and wealth. We do not know what turned Saxton's attention to surveying, but as Seckford took the greatest interest in promoting that work it may have been his original idea, to which Saxton turned his peculiar genius. Whatever the origin, we find Saxton by about 1570 engaged in making surveys in many parts of England, his expenses probably being paid by Seckford who secured grants for him which served in lieu of salary. The nature of these grants is seen in the first one when in 1573, the Crown granted to Saxton the Manor of Grigston, Suffolk, "for certain good causes grand charges and expenses lately had and sustained in the survey of divers parts of England." The grant was for a period of twenty-one years and he paid a rental of £10.5.11; as he collected all the various manorial dues and taxes there would be a substantial income left to him after paying the rent. In 1575 he was appointed "receiver" of the Hospital of St. John of Jerusalem in England, and in 1580 the further grant of land in the parish of St. Sepulchre, London, for 60 years at a nominal rental of three shillings and four pence, with permission to build one or more houses, extended his resources.

From documents in the Public Record Office it is possible to learn something of the methods he used in making his surveys, and this can be supplemented by a critical study of his maps; this we shall attempt to do for Yorkshire. He travelled himself over most of the country depicted on his maps, visiting view points, collecting local information and making innumerable records of the compass bearings from one place to another. In a letter of introduction given to facilitate his survey of Wales in 1576 we see something of this method. The letter reads:

An open letter to all Justices of the Peace, mayors and others, etc. within the severall Shieres of Wales . . . That the said Justices shall be aiding and assisting unto him to see him conducted into any towre Castle highe place or hill to view that countrey and that he may be accompanied with ij or iij honest men such as do best know the countrey for the better accomplishement of that service and that at his departure from any towne or place that he hath taken the view of the said towne do set forth a horseman that can speke both Welshe and englishe to safe conduct him to the next market Towne . . . .

Similar letters were issued in England so that we can picture him setting out on his journey, arriving at the market town, presenting his letter, and being solemnly conducted to the church tower by some of the older men of the town. These men would name for him the hills, villages, rivers and streams and all the prominent features composing the view. Christopher would take his accurate compass bearings to the various objects, ask and record the distances or make his own estimate. The course of streams and some of the other features could be sketched on his rough map and a number of viewpoints selected from which hidden detail might become visible.

There must have been many interesting conferences, arousing much curiosity on the part of his informers, and so Christopher would soon develop the skill of a good chairman, to control the wordy and wandering reminiscences of his guides, otherwise he would never have completed his work at the speed he accomplished. Although this method sounds tedious, he seems to have worked at a great rate when one remembers that he set out into unmapped country and yet correlated innumerable compass bearings, estimated distances and sketched details on to maps which are still surprising in their accuracy.

His engraved and printed maps began to appear in 1575, mainly of the counties of the south and south-west; by 1576 he had worked his way north, and Durham, Cumberland and Westmorland were published, and probably Northumberland also, though this sheet is undated. Yorkshire followed in 1577, but by this time the idea of an atlas of the whole country had been formulated, and the rest of the counties and Wales were completed in 1578. In 1577 he was given an exclusive licence for ten years, to print and publish the maps, and in this document it is stated that he, *hathe already traveyled throughe the greateste parte of this oure Realme of Englande and hathe to the greate pleasure and commoditie of us and oure lovinge subjectes . . . . drawne oute and sett forthe divers trewe and pleasaunte mappes chartes or platts of the same counties Together withe the Cities Townes Villages and ryvers . . .* In 1579 these various county maps were gathered together into the *Atlas of England and Wales*.

In this atlas Yorkshire is drawn on two sheets, each 14″ x 20⅛″ and the scale is approximately three and a half miles to one inch. The title is in a very elaborate cartouche in the top right-hand corner, and in the sea around it there are ships and a spouting whale, while other ships and monsters appear in the Humber and in Bridlington Bay. The coat of arms of Thomas Seckford are in the bottom left-hand corner with the scale and Saxton's name in the bottom right.

Rivers are shown on the map by a very wide line, and the important bridges are put in. Towns are shown by a church and some other buildings, villages by a church only, while hills stand up rather like children's mud pies, and are coloured either green or brown, indiscriminately. The hills provide some further confirmation of his method of working; at many points on the map some hill most noticeably overtops all others in its region, even though in fact it may not be the highest hill. These exaggerated hills mark places of especial importance in Saxton's work. Some are beacons marked with a special symbol such as Penhill Beacon, in Wensleydale; others mark the source of rivers as in the case of Cam Hill

(Camm Fell) the source of the Ribble. Some of them are outstanding hills, such as Ingleborough and Penyghent, though Whernside is omitted altogether, and Wharnside Hill (Great Whernside) behind Kettlewell, included as a giant almost.

Among the small hills promoted to undue importance is Whelpstone Crag, south of Settle. If Saxton climbed this hill he would have a very wide view and could sketch in and get compass bearings for part of Bowland, the Ribble valley around Settle, parts of the Wenning, and the Ingleborough massif. This idea receives some support from the fact that the detail is generally more abundant and more accurate around these hills which are given special prominence.

Holwick Crag, near Middleton-in-Teesdale, is one such point, and the parts of Teesdale around it are shown with very great accuracy. Roseberry Topping (called by Saxton, "Ounsbury toppin hill") is given similar prominence in the North Riding. The spelling on the map shows often that Saxton is going by the sound of names he was told, and names he uses are only approximations, as for instance, in upper Wharfedale, Rasmyll, for Raisegill, and Hawtongill for Halton Gill.

His maps show no roads, but, as remarked already, all the important bridges are shown and a traveller would see how to go from any town or village to the nearest bridge, where he could be directed to the place he wanted. The value of the map in his time is shown by the fact that for nearly a century, his basic surveys were re-drawn and re-issued under many names, but in outline the maps remain essentially the surveys of Saxton. The map of Yorkshire was re-printed on four occasions—by Webb, in 1645; by Phillip Lea, in 1690 and 1699, and by Wildey about 1720.

John Ogilby's Measuring Wheel

THE last chapter brought us up to the publication of Saxton's great map of Yorkshire in 1577, actually the first map of the county. This map continued to be reprinted and Saxton's work based upon his own actual survey continued to be used as the basis of many later maps.

Of the editions of Saxton's map one of the most interesting is that prepared for the 6th edition of Camden's great work descriptive of Britain, and this map was re-engraved from Saxton's original by William Hole. Hole was born at Bramley, near Leeds, and became a famous engraver, particularly of portraits, and his works include engravings of famous and aristocratic persons, Charles I, Henry Prince of Wales, and many of their contemporaries. He was also interested in the engraving of music, and was the first person in England to engrave music on copper plates, the rare music of *Parthenia* being his, and also the *Fantasies of Three Parts,* thought to be composed by Orlando Gibbons. Hole was working in London from 1600 to 1646, and in 1607 published the Saxton map of Yorkshire along with those of several other counties and the title page, for Camden.

Further copies of Saxton were printed in 1610 and 1637, and with altered dates, fresh titles or ornaments, and minor alterations continued to be re-issued until 1770.

The next county map with which we are concerned was made by John Speed in 1610. Speed was the son of a tailor, born at Farndon, Cheshire, in 1552, and was himself a tailor, was admitted a member of the Merchant Tailors' Company in 1580.

Speed showed a great interest in the antiquities of his own county and this attracted the attention of Sir Fulke Greville, who after a time gave him an allowance sufficient to enable him to devote his full energies to these studies and to making a map of the county. He began the preparation of an atlas of county maps similar to that of Saxton, using Saxton's maps as a basis, and indeed, in most details making a frank copy of them. He followed much the same method of work as Saxton, visiting towns and villages and good viewpoints, but still using similar signs on the map for bridges, villages, hills, etc. Some few additions were made and the quality of his work is high. In this quality he was greatly helped by his engraver, Jodocus Hondius, the son of a Flemish engraver who was a refugee in London. In 1594 Hondius went to Amsterdam and there became known to the great cartographer Mercator, and later found a position on his staff.

The maps made by Speed have a similar scale to Saxton's and are issued in two sheets, the North and East Ridings being on one sheet. A new feature which Speed was the first to introduce in this county was to show on the maps the division of the Ridings into their constituent "Hundreds," or "Wapentakes." The interest of the maps was increased by engraving around the maps, in the vacant areas, the coats of arms or portraits of the most important historical figures connected with the county. The map of Lancashire, for instance, has around it: *The portraitures of all those kings sprunge from ye royall families of Lancaster and Yorke which with variable successe got and enjoyed ye Crown and kingdom. This first syde of his mapp of Lancashire (the west) showeth them of Lancaster, the other syde them of the house of York.* On the map those of York are Edward IV, Edward V, Richard III, and Elizabeth.

Speed's maps of Yorkshire were issued in 1610 and are three in number—"Yorke Shire. Performed by John Speed and are to be solde in Popes head alley, against the Exchange by John Sudbury and G. Humble. Cum Privilegio, 1610."

The scale of this map is nearly five miles to an inch; the second is, "The West Ridinge of Yorkeshyre with the most famous and fayre Citie of Yorke described . . ." scale approximately four miles to an inch; the third is "The North and East Ridins of Yorkshire . . . " scale four miles to an inch. These three maps are taken from an atlas of all the counties, *"The Theatre of the Empire of Greate Britaine . . ."*

The ornamentation is limited on the general map of the county to the Royal Arms, scale of miles and title cartouche, but in the map of the West Riding, in addition to the Royal Arms there is a fine plan of the city of York with a list of street names, and also the coats of arms of the Dukes of York since the Norman Conquest. On the map of the North and East Ridings there are plans of Hull and Richmond and the arms of the various Earls of Richmond and Earls of Holderness. In the sea off the coast near Whitby there is the emerging head of a sea monster, a sword-fish just north of Flamborough Head, and a full-rigged ship in Bridlington Bay and in the Humber.

The details of the drawing on the maps are almost identical with Saxton—towns are shown by a church and a few buildings, most villages by a church only, rivers, bridges and parks are shown in the same way and the hills are similar, though fewer in number, and with far greater prominence given to the prominent ones. Those hills which Saxton depicted as outstanding, even though they may not have been the highest were still shown by Speed as far greater than all the rest. This is clearly seen in the West Riding, where on the west of the area, there are five hills standing up well above all the others, like veritable mountains, and these are: Cam Hill, Wharnside Hill (near Kettlewell), Ingleboro' Hill, Pennygent Hill, Whelpston Hill (Bowland Knotts) and Pinnow Hill (near Cononley). Similarly in the other Ridings, the hills selected by Saxton are given further emphasis by Speed.

The two sketches accompanying will show these differences, and it will also be noted that Speed cuts out a great number of the smaller hills. In fact, Saxton seemed to use these small hill signs more or less as a regular pattern over all hilly

country. The faithful copying of Saxton is seen in the drawing of Malham Tarn at the foot of Penyghent, both position and shape being alike on the two maps. The rivers in Saxton's map also have many more small meanders than in Speed's drawing but their lines are similar.

By introducing a larger scale of miles in some of his maps, Speed was able to add some detail to Saxton's mapping, and as his work was equally careful and accurate the resultant maps achieved a high standard and reputation and were constantly re-issued and re-printed during the next 150 years.

Up to the middle of the seventeenth century, maps were almost all issued in atlases with a large number of maps either of countries or of counties bound together, and were essentially intended for the library and for the gentleman's study. Before a journey they may have been consulted but it is most unlikely, by reason of their style and size, that they were ever carried on an actual journey in the way we should carry a map today. The vital change in the character and use of maps came through the work of another surveyor, or rather publisher, John Ogilby, expressed in his road maps.

In the sixteenth century we find the beginnings of another story, for some time running parallel to, but later converging upon and influencing the methods and technique of the map-makers. In 1572, five years before Saxton's map of Yorkshire, Grafton produced a book, *An abridgement of the Chronicles of Englande,* and at the end of the book ten pages are devoted to a table of roads intended to help the traveller to find his way about the country and the principal places of the chronicles. A year earlier, Hollinshed's *Chronicle* had included Harrison's *Description of Britain,* and in this there is a section on roads, "How a man may journey from any noteable towne in England to the citie of London . . . etc." One of these routes is that from Berwick via York to London, and the way is given in moderate and usable detail.

Several "road books" appeared both here and on the continent, following on similar lines, usually small and handy for the traveller and meant for use on the road and not only for the library. In this country the road books were lifted into prominence, and new dignity and significance were bestowed upon them by Ogilby.

John Ogilby was born near Edinburgh in 1600 and grew up to experience remarkable vicissitudes of fortune and to exploit a most varied career. After spending some time as a dancing master he became a theatre owner, then a bookseller and printer. His position as an educated man is indicated by the fact of his authorship of several translations from the classics. Besides his varied professions he had many reverses of fortune to face, being twice completely ruined, first in the Irish rebellion of 1641, when he lost all his money, and later, when his business in London was well established, the Great Fire of 1666 destroyed his house and all his stock which as he was then a printer and bookseller was considerable. None the less, in spite of misfortune he made for himself a name as a surveyor, and was one of four men appointed by the Corporation of London to survey the areas destroyed by the Great Fire. These four prepared a detailed plan of London on the scale of twenty-five inches to the mile, and this was later published (in 1677) by W. Morgan a year after the death of Ogilby.

At some period Ogilby conceived the idea of a new kind of road book which would depict the roads of the kingdom in pictorial form, and for this purpose he employed surveyors to traverse the various roads, to make careful measurements of all distances, note all branch roads and road junctions, and all features of interest near the road. His scheme had the approval of Charles II. In preparation for this publication, seventy-three roads were surveyed and accurately measured; the small illustrations which embellish the titles of the plates in the finished work include some of his surveyors at work with the road-wheel.

This is an instrument resembling the front wheel of a bicycle in its forks, with the wheel geared to a comptometer so that as the surveyor pushes the wheel along the road in front of him, distances are measured and shown on the measuring dial; thus every road described had been walked throughout and the information about cross-roads, bridges, junctions and all the other incidental information was based upon accurate observation. Ogilby used for his measurements the Statute mile, introduced by Act of Parliament in 1593, but not generally adopted until very much later, the old English Customary mile being used on milestones even to the early days of the turnpikes.

The information gathered by Ogilby's surveyors was set out in strip maps and engraved on a hundred folio plates which together made up his road book, *Britannia Depicta,* published in 1675. Each plate of the atlas has a title in the top centre—e.g., "The Road from York to West Chester by John

Ogilby Esq., His Masties. Cosmographer. Containing 106 Miles 4 Furlongs vizt. . . ." Then follow details of the distances from one important town to the next, then "with a Branch from Manchester to Derby Terminating Plate the Second."

The plates are divided into vertical strips drawn to look like a continuous spiral scroll flattened; the road with its minor bends is drawn down this, but at all major changes of direction there is a compass dial to show the changing orientation of the strip. Towns and villages are named, miles distance are written against the road, bridges are shown and named and the destination of side roads is given. Some of the larger natural features such as hills or deep valleys—e.g., Holden Clough, and open moors, Herchet Moor between Halifax and Liversedge, are also named, though it is by no means a constant practice. Villages and larger houses and country seats which come within the width of the strip, generally about a mile on each side of the road, are also included.

Although Ogilby's Atlas was not small enough to be carried on a journey, its information was presented in a clear and concise form which could be copied or noted with little difficulty or the plates could be torn out of the atlas on occasions of emergency. The form of the strip map has remained in use with modifications until the present day, and most of us must have cycled at one time or another, following such a route map, perhaps with the addition of a profile and modern road signs.

On this matter of road information one other thing might find mention at this point. One of the early cartographers was John Norden, whose work was mainly confined to the south and east of England. We owe to him, however, the invention of the triangular table of distances, which is still used in many ways, the commonest being the bus and tramway fare stage-tables. The towns along a road are written in a vertical column downwards from the starting point, then written horizontally across the top in the same order. In each space of the rectangular mesh formed by drawing horizontal and vertical lines between the town names, the distance between the town or the price of the fare between the stages shown at the side and top of the columns which form the space by their intersection, is shown. This device of Norden's rapidly became popular and was added to the road books and in some cases to the maps.

The details of the roads on Ogilby's plates were so clear and precise that it was an easy matter for an engraver to draft any of them on to an existing map, and in the next group of maps we shall consider, there are many examples of this practice where the addition of one or two of Ogilby's roads on to a Saxton or Speed base-map, has been the principal advance.

Maps on Playing Cards

SPEED'S work in Yorkshire added little to the original survey of Saxton beyond printing separately the maps of the Ridings, adding the boundaries of the "Hundreds" and slightly amending the detail in a few points. Ogilby with his *Britannia,* in 1675 made the next real contribution by his survey of the principal roads, and their publication. There were, however, one or two maps in the period between Speed and Ogilby that ought to be mentioned in passing.

In 1626, an abridgement of Camden's *Britannia; a Chorographical Description . . .* was made, and this included maps of all the counties drawn by John Bill. These were small maps, only 4½" x 3¼", but were quite clear and attractive and the simplification was cleverly done. The one outstanding new feature was the inclusion along the margins of the latitude and longtitude, though the latter is based upon the old zero meridian out in the Atlantic. In their main features these maps were copies based on those of Peter Keer, made between 1599 and 1620, and in no way were they a re-survey.

In 1636 a Dutch engraver, Johan Janssen, produced a copy of Speed and Saxton, beautifully engraved and usually very skilfully coloured, and with a scale of approximately four miles to an inch. Another Dutch engraver and publisher, Johan Blaeu, followed suit in 1645 with a copy of Speed, but Blaeu and Janssen only competed to produce better copies of existing maps. Theirs are among the most popular coloured maps of the county today.

From 1620 to the end of the century, Mercator, Speed and Saxton maps were being re-printed with little alteration except occasionally in a re-drawn title, and Blaeu and Janssen also re-printed their maps in new editions of their various atlases so that there was a steady re-printing of one or other almost every year. As Camden remained the standard work on popular history and topography of the county, new editions were frequently printed with re-prints of the Saxton maps, until in 1670 a new map engraver appears in Richard Blome.

Blome was a cartographer and publisher of books of heraldry and topography, having a shop in London between the years 1668 and 1679. He published a *Geographic Description of the four parts of the world* in 1670, and in 1673 completed *Britannia, a Geographic Description of the kingdom of England, Scotland and Ireland.* This was based on Camden and had county maps among which are three for Yorkshire: one of the whole county approximately six miles to the inch; one of the West Riding, and one of the North and East Ridings. These were only very poor copies of Saxton and Speed and, in fact, all his work, both maps and text, was of poor quality and most of it was pirated.

At last, with Robert Morden, something new in maps of the counties appeared. Morden was a map and globe maker at the Atlas, Cornhill, London, working about 1668, and twenty years later was in partnership with another map printer, Thomas Cockerill.

In 1676 Morden produced a pack of playing cards, *The 52 Counties of England and Wales, described in a pack of cards. . . .* The cards are $2\frac{1}{8}''$ by $2''$ and have at the top the name of the county, with the suit and the number occupying about a quarter of the card. The bottom quarter has a few particulars of the county, length, breadth and latitude of the principal town with its distance from London. The rest of the card has a small map of the county and, in the case of Yorkshire, two roads are transferred from Ogilby's survey so that this becomes the first county map to indicate any roads. One road is via Doncaster-Wetherby-York-Yarm and so to Durham, the other is Rotherham-Wakefield-Otley-Richmond and so north. In the next few years there were many re-prints of these cards and the idea was adopted by many publishers with the production of many various sets of cards with maps.

A translation of Camden into English was published in 1695, the translation being by Edmund Gibson, and in this Morden provided the county maps, which are very carefully and cleverly engraved. The latitude and longitude is included and now the longitude is related to the new meridian through

Greenwich. On the map of the North Riding all Ogilby's roads are included but not on those of the other Ridings. In 1701, Morden issued a second set of independent county maps, smaller than those in Camden $8\frac{1}{4}''$ by $6\frac{1}{2}''$, for the West Riding and the North and East Ridings together. These maps have all Ogilby's roads inserted.

We can perhaps say, at this point, that all through the seventeenth century the maps had appeared either as leaves bound together in large library atlases or as illustrations in Camden or other similar topographical works. The loose and separate map of a county was still almost unknown, but with the eighteenth century the separate survey and loose map was to appear.

In 1711, however, the old tradition was continued by Sutton Nichols with his *New Map of Yorkshire with the Post and Cross Roads,* five miles to an inch, and a sheet $18\frac{1}{4}''$ by $14\frac{1}{8}''$. This was actually a copy of Janssen's map of 1646 with Ogilby's roads inserted on it.

At the very end of the century, Ogilby's road maps were supplemented by a new road book, that of Paterson, which was to remain in popular and general use with extensions, revisions and re-printings for a century and a half. James Paterson re-wrote Ogilby in an amended form, under the title:

> *The Traveller's Guide: a most exact Description of the Roads of England. Being Mr. Ogilby's Actual Survey and Mensuration by the Wheel of the Great Roads to all the Considerable Cities and Towns in England and Wales, together with the Cross Roads from one City or Eminent Town to another. . . . Wherein is Shown the Distance from Place to Place and plain Directions given to find the way, by setting down every Town, Village, River, Brook, Bridge, Common, Forest, Wood, Copse, Heath, Moor, etc., that occur in passing the Roads. And for the better Illustration thereof there are added Tables wherein the Names of the Places with their Distances, are set down in Column, in so plain a manner that a meer Stranger may Travel all over England without any other Guide.*

This marks the new tradition, to cater for the solitary traveller and help him to find his way about the country, and Paterson's *Roads,* as it was known, went through eleven editions in the century, and was then considerably enlarged and re-published by Mogg. In 1826 it was in its eighteenth edition, with entirely new maps as an appendix.

Paterson's work was a fitting introduction to the new map by Warburton. John Warburton published a new survey of Northumberland in 1716, and by 1718 was at work on a map of Yorkshire which he completed and published in 1720. At the time he started the Yorkshire survey he was employed as a supervisor of Excise at Bedale, but was in some sort of trouble, and for this reason and for the purpose of his survey asked for leave of absence for a few months, and this was granted. The idea of a new map of Yorkshire had been discussed with Thoresby, the Leeds antiquary, and many letters passed between them concerning the survey. The map was designed to be on a new and larger scale than any previously done, five miles to two inches, printed on four sheets, with three supplementary sheets with title and drawings of coats of arms. It seems certain that Warburton employed a surveyor who traversed most of the roads of Yorkshire, except the ones given in greatest detail by Ogilby, and that distances were checked with the wheel.

Warburton and his assistants ascended church towers and took bearings and distances exactly as Saxton and Speed had done, and also traversed roads and compiled survey notes of the houses and other buildings and places of importance along the road and to each side of it. His methods of work have been admirably studied by W. B. Crump (Thoresby Soc. Miscellanea. Vol. 28, 1928) and many of his letters and notes from his journal have been printed.

Warburton's chief job was the securing of subscribers to his map, and to help in this he included the coat of arms of 693 of the county gentry on the supplementary sheets. He seems to have had introductions from one gentleman to another, to have been received at their houses in his peregrination of the county and to have made drawings of their houses. In his journeys around Leeds and Wharfedale he stayed at Ripley Castle and was kindly received and entertained and saw some rare manuscripts. He lodged with Thoresby in Leeds, stayed at Weston Hall, Aldborough Hall, and many other places.

The map was engraved and printed and supplied to the subscribers in 1720 under the elaborate title of:

"A New and Correct Map of the County of York in all its Divisions. By Actual Survey and dimensuration: with the Arms and Seats of the Nobility and Gentry, the Distances in

Miles and Furlongs between each of the Market Towns. The courses of the several Roman Ways, Present Roads, Rivers and Rivulets, Churches, Cast. Religs. House, Ancnt. Baronies, Forests, Chases, Parks, Woods, Mountains, Lakes, Fields of Battle, Collieries, Copper Mines, Allom Works, or other Minerals, Sea Coast, Rocks, Sands, Shoals, &c. By John Warburton, Esq., Somerset Herald of Arms, and Fellow of the Royal Society. Engraven by S. Parker. Four sheets, each about 24½″ x 18⅜″.

The map is divided into two-inch squares (ten miles) and these are numbered on the top margin 1 to 25 and lettered down the left A to T (the J omitted), a method of quick reference used in many later maps and in modern atlases and maps. In the top margin also is "Minutes of Time from London." On the south margin is a division into degrees and minutes of longitude, and on the east margin, degrees, minutes, and twenty seconds of latitude. The longitude is, however, very inaccurate. The line of the meridian of London is correctly shown passing through Flamborough Head, but the line of 1° West passes through Otley and Richmond instead of through York, and this mistake is repeated in most maps for the next fifty years, although Morden had already published maps with the correct longitude upon them.

Of the detail on Warburton's map, that of the additional roads beyond those of Ogilby is, at least in part, where Warburton had new surveys made, very valuable, as is also his noting of the line of the Roman roads. His detail of hills and rivers in the west of the map is poor and often wrong. Distance shown on the map between market towns is given both in computed and measured miles.

A letter of Thoresby's gives a clue to the reason for the great rarity of copies of this map. He says, "I question not, but you have heard of Mr. Warburton's noble Map of Yorkshire. The Arms of the Nobility and Gentry are to be engraved on each side, as in that he has done of Northumberland, which is not to be got for money, he having stuck to his promise that none shall have any Map but Subscribers . . ." This seems to have been the procedure in Yorkshire, with the result that very few copies are known. Bradford Public Reference Library has two copies, the Bodleian, British Museum and Cambridge University Libraries have copies, and there are probably three others in private hands in Yorkshire. It must be that there are copies or odd sheets unrecognised in some of the private houses and libraries of

Yorkshire. This will remain an important reference map for the state of the roads and particularly the Roman roads at the beginning of the eighteenth century.

A very interesting set of maps was issued four years after Warburton's, by Herman Moll, a Dutchman, who had come to London in 1688, and was a friend of the famous antiquary Dr. Stukely. Moll set up in business as a geographer and bookseller, and in 1724 published a still further addition to the long list of *New Description of England and Wales . . . &c* to which he added *a new and correct set of Maps of each County . . . . and to render 'em the more acceptable to the Curious, their Margins are Adorn'd with great Variety of very remarkable Antiquities . . . &c.*

It was probably his great friendship with Stukeley that induced Moll to take up this interest and to make his maps doubly interesting. For Yorkshire there are four maps, Yorkshire with the Post Roads, etc., the West Riding, the East Riding and the North Riding. Each is oblong, approximately $9\frac{1}{2}''$ by $7\frac{1}{8}''$ the map leaving a wide margin at the two ends, and these margins filled with drawings and notes. The map of Yorkshire has a curious old drawing of the Devil's Arrows at Boroughbridge, with a plan showing the position of the fourth, which had disappeared. There are three drawings of Roman inscribed stones from York, and a Roman urn.

The West Riding map has on the left of it, Roman remains from Adel, Boroughbridge, and York, and on the right a description of the gibbet at Halifax. The East Riding Map has figures of Saxon coins, and the North Riding has Saxon coins and Roman inscriptions. The maps themselves are very clear, carefully engraved and show roads which are, in the main, copied from Warburton, and the whole set of fifty were re-printed the same year without the description of Britain, while the description of Britain with all the maps was re-printed again in 1728.

We might close this chapter conveniently with a small map printed in 1741, again as illustration in a "description"—*Chorographia Britanniae or a set of Maps of all the Counties in England and Wales . . .* by Thomas Badeslade, engraved by W. H. Toms. This map is only $4\frac{1}{8}''$ by $5\frac{1}{8}''$ with an inch and a half margin down the west side. The map is neat, but with the rivers very much exaggerated, no hills or natural features are shown, and only a selection of towns. Three main roads are shown, the first running from south to north, entering the county near Tickhill, through Doncaster, Pontefract, Sherborne, Tadcaster, Boroughbridge, and Northallerton and so to Darlington. From this road there is a branch to Scarborough. There is a short road from Hull via Beverley to Bridlington and Flamborough. The third road is by Sheffield, Barnsley, Huddersfield, upper Wharfedale and over Coverdale Head to Middleham and Richmond and on to Barnard Castle.

The column on the left of the map lists the boroughs and describes the divisions of the county into Ridings, with one city, 13 Boroughs, 46 other Market Towns, 563 Parishes, and sends 30 Members to Parliament. The list of boroughs gives market day and the number of members sent to Parliament. On the first edition Leeds is not mentioned in the list, but in the re-print of 1742 it is included at the end in the brief note, "Leeds, a Cloth Fair, Market Tues. and Sat." In fact the boroughs at that time include none of our present larger towns, the thirteen, with two Members of Parliament each, being perhaps of interest—Aldborough, Beverley, Boroughbridge, Heydon, Kingston-upon-Hull, Knaresborough, Malton, Northallerton, Pontefract, Richmond, Ripon, Scarborough, and Thirsk.

Annotated Maps

WE have seen that during the early years of the eighteenth century the roads depicted by Ogilby and described by Paterson were being united to the basic surveys of Saxton and Warburton, and this union we can regard as the beginning of a new period and style of map-making. Maps were no longer meant primarily to ornament the library of the private gentleman, but were intended for a wider travelling public, and were now to be used as guides and informants on the way and on all matters of interest near to the road being travelled. This popular trend is also seen in the large numbers of maps which were being re-printed and published in such regularity for the London booksellers, as well as those appearing in publications such as the Universal Magazine and other periodicals.

Moll's maps of 1724, as described earlier, introduced the wider field of archaeological interest in the pictures of various objects drawn alongside the map. The archaeological world was stimulated in 1736 by the production, in his history of the city of York, of Drake's map of the Roman roads of the county. The map is inscribed, "To the Society of Antiquaries in London, this Plate of the Roman Roads in the County of York, etc." Its scale is approximately seven miles per inch, and little except the Roman roads is shown. These are less accurate than the ones drawn on Warburton's map, and do not represent an actual survey but only a compilation and the production of a map with a single specialised interest.

Passing over several engravers who produced small maps of the county and its ridings, two new surveyors appeared about the middle of the century who deserve mention. Thomas

Title piece of Emanuel Bowen's Map of the North Riding.

Two maps of the 17th century.

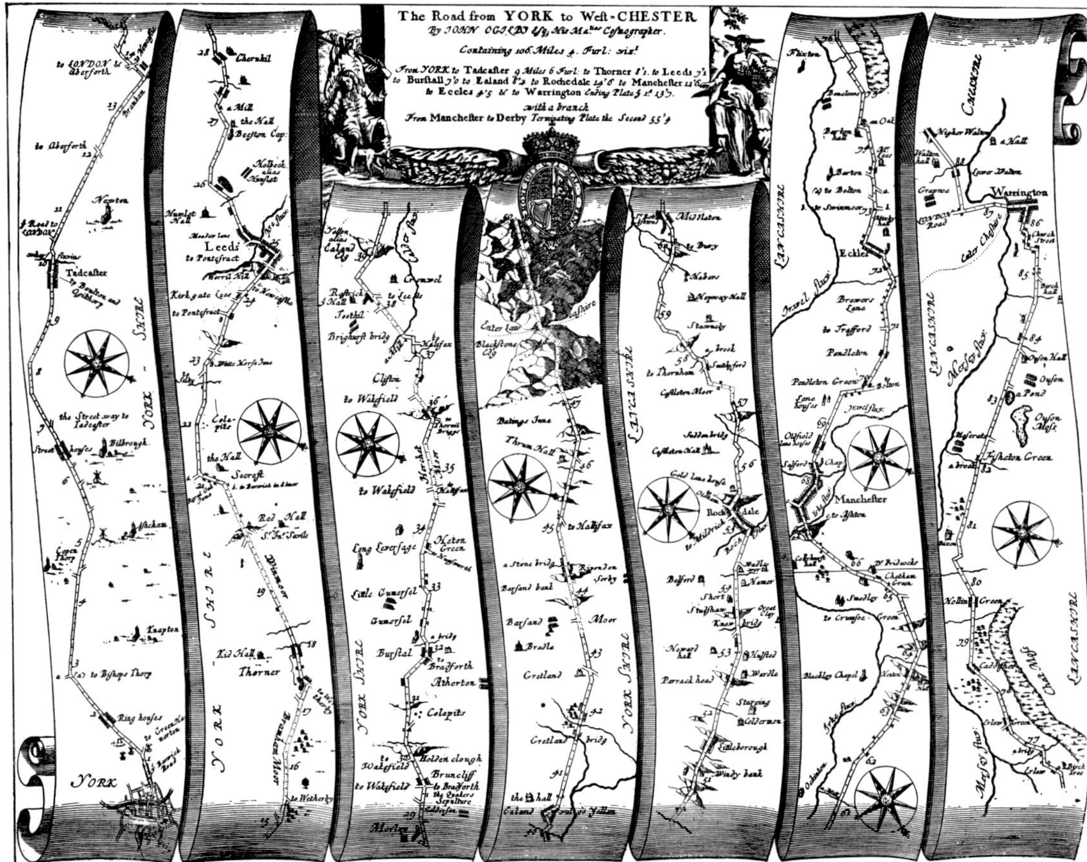

A section of John Ogilby's Strip Map.

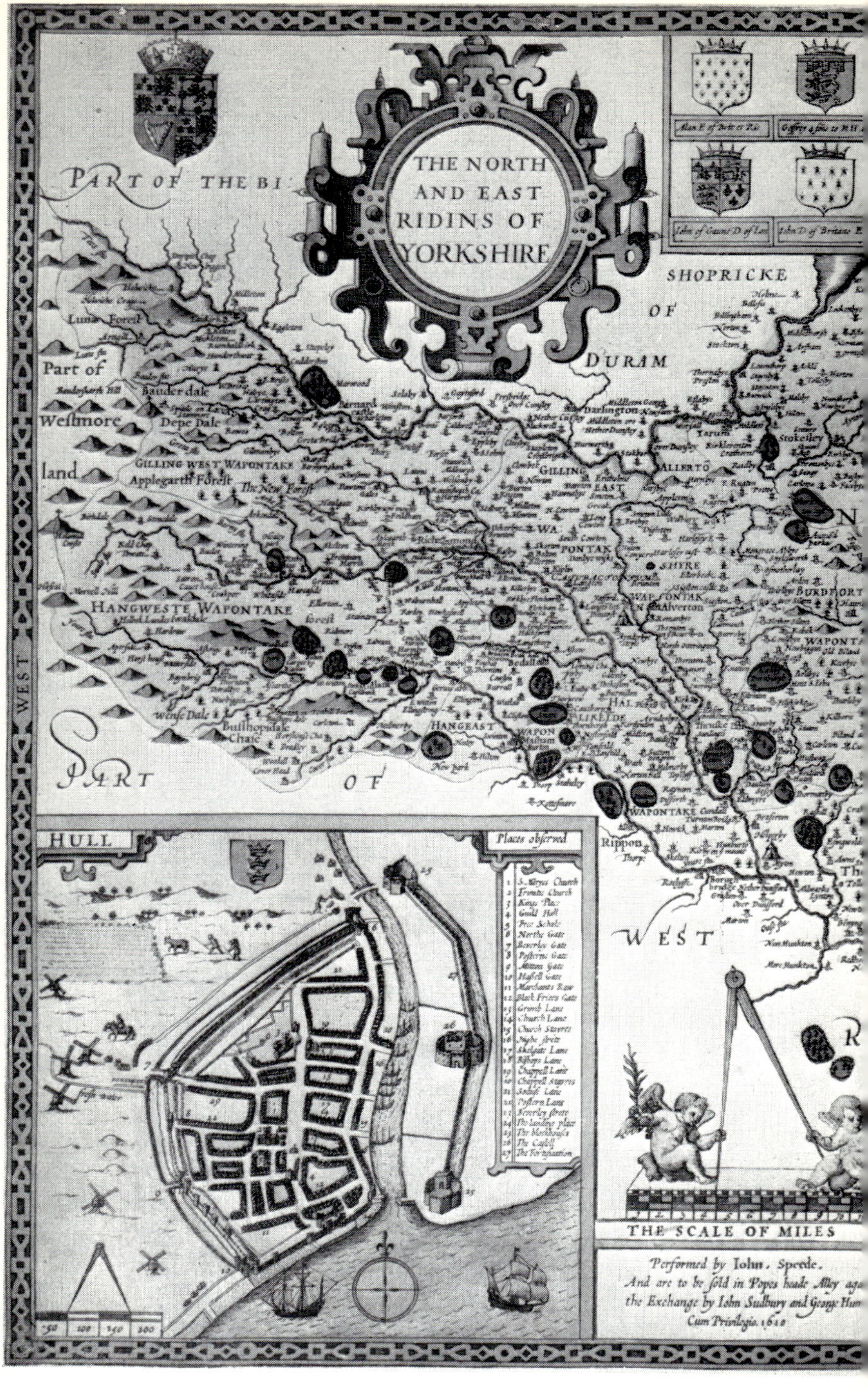

John Speed's map of the North and

ns'' of Yorkshire, published in 1610.

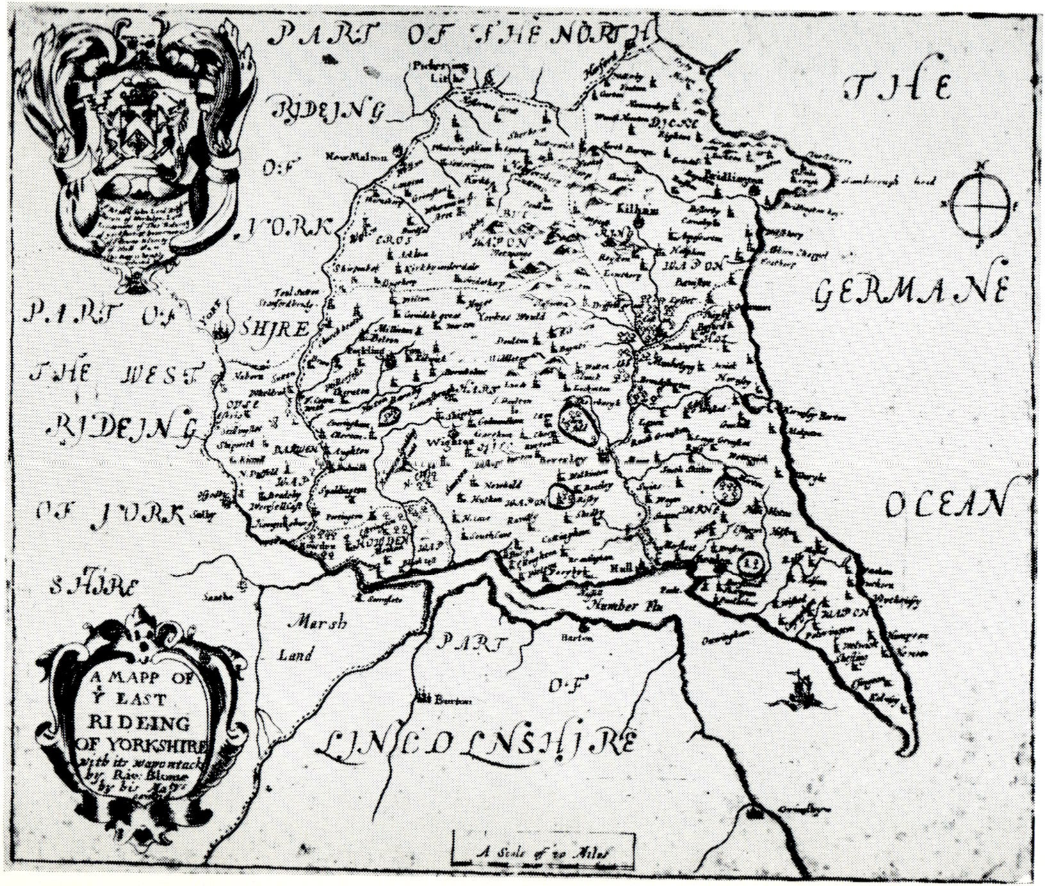

An early map
of the East
Riding.

JOHN METCALF AGED 78.

Drawn by J. R. Smith.

Published as the Act directs Aug.t 31. 1795 by E & R Peck York

Book illustration of the Blind Surveyor.

A portion of Jefferys' Map showing Langstrothdale and Beckermonds.

Kitchin produced his first maps of the county in 1749, and went on with new and different editions until 1794. He was an engraver and publisher and also hydrographer to the King, and produced some very clearly-engraved and accurate maps of the separate ridings which, according to their title, are "Drawn from an Actual Survey and Regulated by Astronl. Observations." The first set of rather small maps, around eight to twelve miles to the inch, was prepared for and published in the *London Magazine or Gentleman's Monthly Intelligencer*. Vol. XVIII.

Some of Kitchin's maps are most attractive for their titles, which are carried on a scroll supported by a fragment of classical architecture and with various objects displayed at the foot of it. The map of the North Riding has the scroll surmounted by the arms of the city of York, and below it, a crossed sword and mace. Behind the support is seen a wide prospect of countryside with a town with large buildings and a spired church.

Kitchin's map of Cumberland issued at the same time has a drawing of two men working a "jack-roller," drawing a skip of coals from a mine shaft, and in the background a basket of poultry prepared for market, with two very large birds in front of it, pecking food from the ground. The map of Durham has a "still life" group of three barrels labelled "mustard seed," a large fish-hook, two sacks of some commodity, and a scoop, with tall growing plants each side of the scroll and a ship in the far background.

The most interesting map at the middle of the century was that prepared by Emanuel Bowen, engraver and publisher, of London. In 1720 he had published two small maps, one of the North and East Ridings and one of the West Riding, to be included in a re-print of Ogilby, but in 1750 he produced his large maps, four in number, and of a new type, and approximately 27 inches by 20 inches. These maps are very clearly engraved, and incorporate a great amount of detail based largely on Warburton, with latitude and longitude corrected, and the maps divided into squares of 15 minutes. The new feature of the maps is the wealth of comment inscribed on them, which gives a brief epitome of the more interesting and curious lore of some of the towns and villages. These comments are themselves very curious and entertaining and some of them might be worthy of quotation here.

The first map of the series is one of the whole county very nearly on a scale of five miles to an inch. York is taken as the centre and concentric rings at one-mile intervals are inscribed over the whole area. The comments on this map are mainly lists of the Earls and Dukes of York and Richmond and of the seats of the nobility and gentry, though one paragraph gives some statistical account of the county, saying that it is much the largest in England, giving its length and breadth, and that there are 3,770,000 acres, 26 Wapentakes, one city, 13 boroughs, 57 market towns, 563 parishes, and about 106,160 houses; it would be interesting to know how this last figure was arrived at or estimated.

The title of the map is, as usual, drawn on a bold architectural monument, with a horse at one side and cattle at the other. In front of it there are many objects typifying the county—a spinning-wheel, sheep and shears, a large basket of bottled Scarborough Spa water, scythe, sickle and corn, anvil and hammer, saddle and harness, wool-comb and a pile of cloth pieces.

The East Riding map has a second small map inserted in the top right-hand corner and labelled, "An Epitomised Map of the East Riding of Yorkshire in its several Divisions by Referential Letters, By a Gentleman Residing in the County," though its purpose is not made clear. The general title to the map has an impressive spring-head, presumably the spa well at some place in the Riding. On one side of the spring there is a fishing-rod, creel and some fish, on the other side a heap of cheeses and a man working a large press. We are told that, "the East Riding has such a competancy of the conveniences and necessaries of life as to render the Situation of the industrious Inhabitants very eligible. Although the Air cannot be supposed to be free of Noxious Vapours, yet this inconvenience is fully recompensed by the fruitfulness of the Soil near the Sea, and the Trade that is carried on by the Inhabitants of the Sea-port towns of Bridlington, Hornsey, Patrington and Kingston upon Hull."

After a note on some fossils, "Astroites, which resemble Equisetum or Horse Tail, and which some Naturalists suppose to be rock-plants," he speaks of the rivers and springs, especially the "Gypsies" or intermittent springs of the chalk wolds, which are thought to foretell some bad event when running but are a good omen when dry. He says the Marr-water in the way from Bridlington to Hornsey (Hornsey Mere) is deep and always fresh, and well stocked with pike, perch and eels. There is plenty of pit coal for fuel and no want of turf and wood, the coal being brought by sea.

Of the many paragraphs relating to particular places only a few can be quoted, "Ackham or Accome (Acomb, near York) noted for a Mount called Sivers from Severus, who dying at his Palace at York, his Body was burned here after the Roman manner, and his ashes being put in a Golden Urn, was carried to Rome and laid in the Monument of Antoninus." Severus died in York in the year A.D. 211, in February, and his body was placed on a funeral pyre outside the city, but the actual site has never been authenticated, and Bowen was probably following general tradition as given by Camden and others.

Fulford is described as the scene of a "bloody Battle" between Harald Harfager, King of Norway, and Edwin, Earl of Mercia, etc. Rical, or Richal (Riccal) is the site of another event in the pre-Conquest history, the landing of Harald Haardreada and an account of his defeat by Harold, King of England, is given.

The notes on Beverley give some interesting information relating to its buildings and trade—it is the chief town of the Riding, of great antiquity, and is free of tolls in the whole of England. It is constantly supplied with a great plenty of fish, fowl, corn and other provisions. Its trade is chiefly in malt, oat-meal, glue, leather and a large export of all kinds of grains as the Beck had recently been cleared and vessels of larger burden could come right up to the town. A great quantity of bone-lace is made and the trade in it is receiving much encouragement of late. Flixton "is noted for an Hospital built here in the time of Athelstan, to defend Travellers from Wolves, which in those times infested these parts." Bridlington is a place of good trade with a plentiful market. At Hornsey there is a note on coast erosion—"not many years since there was a small Street adjoining to the Sea called Hornsey Beck, which is now almost all washed away by the sea; and, they have here a tradition that a little to the North of this town there was a Village called Hide, long since devoured by the Sea."

On the bottom of the map there is a view of Kingston upon Hull, a fine engraving 10 inches by 2¾ inches, which displays the town along the river side with a river crowded with shipping, and with the pier and the twelve-gun battery clearly drawn. There is a long account of the town under the drawing, starting by saying the town is of no antiquity, being founded by Ed. I.

His description reads in quaint fashion in some parts.

"Their Trade to Iceland for Fish by the Common Stock of the Inhabitants (which being dried and hardened for sale, they call stock Fish) has raised them so great a Treasure as enabled them not only to Fence the Town with a strong Brick wall but to strengthen it with Towers and Bulwarks where it was not defended by the river Hull . . . " At first glance it may seem from the lack of punctuation, that the dried inhabitants are called stock-fish, but this is hardly the intention of the passage. He gives also a long description of the garrison of the town, and of the halls and buildings of the Merchant Adventurers.

These detailed descriptions, along with the engraved views of towns, the Roman roads and forts with their Roman names, and a multitude of other small features, were added to the maps to make them serve a new purpose, the entertainment and guidance of the person of leisure who wished to see the curiosities both natural and artificial of the county over which he travelled. In fact these are really the first maps to become the companion of the intelligent traveller for pleasure, by which he could carry with him on one sheet both a map of the county and an outline historical guide.

The North Riding map has the simplest title, having a gushing well-head with three horses drinking at it, one being ridden by a jockey or postillion guide, the other two by travellers. There is a large basket of bottled Scarborough Spa water, and in the background part of a timbered barn or other building. A view of the city of York is at the bottom and we are told that "the City at this Time for its Magnificence, may be deservedly reckoned the second in the Kingdom." After saying that it is fair, beauteous and populous, he says many of the gentry have their winter houses there and many public assemblies, but the trade is lately much decayed, though there are still many considerable merchants there. As the Riding is rather small, the map leaves large spaces for comment, and this is the richest sheet, so that we can only pick one or two for quotation, although all are entertaining.

"Bolton gives title to his Grace the Duke of Bolton. This place is remarkable for the Birth of Henry Jenkins, who was Born here in 1500 and died at Ellerton upon Swale in 1670. He was 12 years old when the Battle of Flodden field was fought, on Sept. 9th 1513, which he remembered, so that he lived 169 years which was 16 longer than Old Par, and was, says Dr. Tancred Robinson, the oldest Man born upon the Ruins of this Postdiluvian World."

There is a note on the trade of Richmond: "The Market is very plentifully supplied with Cattle and provisions, and is one of the best for Corn in the North of England. It has a good Trade for Stockings and Woollen knit Caps for Seamen; but its Trade of late is greatly improv'd by the encouragement given by the Corporation to industrious Mechanics and Tradesmen of all kinds, from all parts to settle among them . . "

Alum manufacture is noted for Whitby and near Gisbrough, and Whitby has a fleet of a hundred ships, but Robin Hood's Bay is credited as "the most Noted for the Fishing Trade of any in these parts; especially for Crabs and Lobsters, having a peculiar method of keeping them when taken, near the shore, in a Machine they call Hully which is in shape like a great Chest bored full of holes, to let in the Sea, which at High water always overflows it. In it are kept vast quantities of Crabs and Lobsters all the Season, which they take out more or less, according to the quickness or slowness of their Markets . . . . "

Scarborough has a long notice, and among other things we are told that it has a commodious quay and that most of its ships are employed in the Newcastle and London coal trade, and a few in the fishing. "The Spaw belonging to the Town is very famous as well on account of the virtue of the Waters, as for the great resort of Nobility and Gentry who come hither in the season for their diversion. About 12 years since the Craggy Mountain from which the Springs arose, suddenly fell after two or three loud and frightful Cracks; the Buildings over the Wells and Dicky Dickenson's house were buried in the ruins, which altering the course of the Springs and absorbing and swallowing them up in such a manner, that twas a considerable time before they were found again."

The map of the West Riding has a view of Leeds in the top right-hand corner, and the caption mentions the fine stone bridge over the Aire, on which the mixed cloth market was formerly held. The title of the map is surmounted by pieces of cloth and hanks of yarn, a spinning-wheel and winding frame and a shuttle. In front an old woman is carding wool, a girl spinning it, and four children gathering it and selling it to a merchant who packs it in a large sack. There are two mountain streams, and near one of them a case and heap of Sheffield cutlery, cattle and sheep browsing by the other. "The Air of the West Riding is more wholesome than either that of the East or North especially in the upland parts." This should please the present population to contemplate, when accusations are levelled against our dirty woollen districts.

Sheffield, we are told, has about 600 master cutlers each with his own stamp to mark his wares, and 40,000 men are employed in the iron trade of Hallamshire. Beeston, near Leeds, is noted for bone-lace, straw hats and hat bands. Bowen notes the famous quarries of building stone at Huddleston, and of Alabaster at Farburn; Ripon, Knaresborough, Wakefield, Halifax, Selby, and several smaller places have lengthy notes, and all the Roman roads have a little note where they enter the county, as to their name and where they go. The Devil's Causeway is shown from Kirkby Lonsdale to Bainbridge, and a note says it goes forward to Scotland by Barnard Castle. The trade notes are certainly the most interesting at present, and generally unexpected as, for instance, that Doncaster has a good trade in stockings and knitted waistcoats, or Wortley has a good seam of clay from which Leeds artificers make good clay pipes.

Possibly too much time has been given to these maps, but they are certainly among the most entertaining and useful for the local historian, and they will repay study at any time. They were re-printed many times in the next thirty-five years, and are the best maps until the appearance of Jefferys' large survey and atlas of the county in 1771, which must be the subject for a separate chapter. A great many smaller maps and re-prints of earlier ones were also produced during these years, but no advantage would be gained by describing them in detail.

We can perhaps say that Bowen's maps come at the end of the second period of Yorkshire maps; first we had the Saxton-Speed group with their copyists, then the new surveys incorporating Ogilby and Warburton. The third group will be Jefferys' map and survey, and the work of Greenwood, preparatory to the publications of the Ordnance Survey. Somewhere in this group we must find a place for the great engraver Cary and the maps he provided for many purposes, not least the basic map for William Smith's first geological map of the county, which we shall describe later.

A Blind Surveyor

WE have brought the story of the maps and map-makers of the county up to the middle of the eighteenth century, and must now enter upon a period of rapid change and progress in almost every branch of human activity. At the time when Bowen was making his maps, essentially in the old tradition but with the addition of notes to arouse the interest of the traveller, events in the North were bringing to birth the idea and demand which in its development blossomed out into the Ordnance Survey, now the foremost survey and map-making organisation in the world.

The year 1745 saw the rise of the second Jacobite Rebellion and the attempt to foster this rising over the whole country in such a way as to secure the restoration of the Stuart Kings to the throne. The rebellion was defeated by the army led by the Duke of Cumberland, but in his campaign into the Highlands to quell the last efforts of the rebels, his movements were severely hampered and his campaign delayed by ignorance of the country and the entire lack of outside knowledge of the tracks and passes through the mountains. To remove this difficulty and to enable an efficient watch to be kept on the Highland populations, the Government were advised to institute or finance the preparation of an official survey and the printing of a reliable map on a large scale—at least one inch to a mile. In a later chapter we shall follow the development of this demand and the rise of the Ordnance survey.

Shortly after the middle of the century, under the stimulus of the demands of our rapidly-increasing trade, the Royal Society of Arts offered a prize of £100 for the best county maps on a scale of approximately one inch to a mile. Thus, from two angles, official and private, there was an incentive to produce maps with a new degree of accuracy and on a new scale which was to prove the one most generally acceptable for the next 200 years.

The inventions in machinery which had ushered in the period now called the Industrial Revolution, were followed by the rapid development of new towns and centres of trade, and these in turn demanded much more travelling about the country than ever before. Not only was better transport needed for human beings, but the carriage of goods needed better roads or alternative modes of transport. Two responses were made to this impulse, the development of the turnpike roads, and of canals, and each in its way contributed to the advancement and extension of surveys and map-making. Finally, a new branch of detailed surveying was encouraged and, in fact, made essential by the change in agriculture which is expressed in the Enclosure Acts for which ground had to be surveyed on a large scale, re-divided and the new divisions set out, with new lines of road and all other features of land surveying. The product of this demand was the wonderful series of field and township maps attached to the Enclosure Awards and the general progress of what is called cadastral surveys—those dealing with the shape and area of portions of land.

Because it continues the tradition of the road books which we have already mentioned, we might turn first to the new road surveys initiated by the Turnpike Acts. During the sixteenth century, Acts had been passed which made each parish responsible for the highways within it, and in the seventeenth century a hundred years' experience of the inefficiency and abuse of these Acts had led to the first step in establishing roads on a wider responsibility.

The Turnpike Act of 1663 gave power to the County Justices to levy tolls for the upkeep of any length of road, but as this did not prove very satisfactory, the first Turnpike Trust was constituted in 1706. The Trust was administered by a body of commissioners, usually local gentry nominated in a Private Act of Parliament. They were to maintain roads and levy tolls, and usually the Trust was responsible for a main road along the whole of its length between two market towns.

Some of the earliest turnpike roads were connected with the growing textile trade centres of Lancashire and Yorkshire —e.g. 1732, the Manchester to Salterbrook (on the way to

Halifax); 1735, Oldham to West Yorkshire, and Rochdale to Halifax; 1759, Manchester to Huddersfield, and so on. The turnpikes were very unpopular, as local people objected to paying tolls for short journeys from one village to another, and there was a great fear among the farmers that the tolls would restrict their movements between the markets.

In 1753 there was much rioting in West Yorkshire, and serious trouble was experienced at Otley and Harrogate where mobs burned the toll bars and destroyed the gates along the turnpikes.

The extended use of wheeled carriages, goods waggons, and stage coaches made many of the older roads unsuitable because of their steep gradients, so that new lines of road had to be laid out. This involved surveying the proposed routes and determining levels, and surveys of ground for the purchase of land along the route. The most spectacular Yorkshire figure in this connection is that of Blind Jack, to whose skill we owe many hundreds of miles of roads still in use in the county. Although Jack never made a map, he surveyed the line for many roads, and so demands inclusion in any outline of Yorkshire maps and surveyors.

John Metcalfe was born at Knaresborough on the 15th of August, 1717, and was a normal child until the age of six years, when a bout of smallpox left him totally blind. He seems to have been a courageous and clever lad as he soon learned to find his way alone anywhere around Knaresborough, and managed to join other boys in their games and pranks. For ten years he was a leader in mischievous pranks and jests of all kinds, and seemed to suffer very little disability from his blindness. His whole life continued this character for fun and excitement, and is better reading than almost any novel. His adventures are fully recounted in his biography, printed during his lifetime, under the title:-

The life of John Metcalfe, commonly called Blind Jack of Knaresborough. With many Entertaining Anecdotes of his Exploits in Hunting, Card-Playing, &c. Some particulars relative to the Expedition against the Rebels in 1745, *in which he bore a personal share; and also A Succinct Account of his various contracts for Making Roads, Erecting Bridges and other Undertakings in Yorkshire, Lancashire, Derbyshire and Cheshire; which for a series of years have brought him into Public Notice as a most Extraordinary Character.*

This was printed in York in 1795, and is worth anyone's

time to read. His direct connection with roads begins in 1751 when he set up a stage-waggon service between Knaresborough and York, running twice a week in summer and weekly in winter until such time as he took his first road-making contract. This was the turnpike authorised from Harrogate to Boroughbridge, on which he took the making of three miles between Minskip and Fearnsby.

This he followed by building a bridge of 18 feet span at Boroughbridge, and by contracting for a road between Knaresborough and Harrogate. Other road contracts followed in rapid succession, and included portions of the turnpikes between Skipton and Colne, Chapeltown and Leeds, Halifax and Wakefield and many others. For our purpose it is sufficient to mention that Metcalfe made his own surveys and estimates on a method entirely his own, but one which was apparently very reliable and efficient. He surveyed and traversed all the ground, used his staff as a sounding rod, felt the materials, and laid out some excellent lines on good foundations. He was one of the first road-makers to traverse boggy ground with a safe road, and both roads and bridges which he surveyed and constructed remain to this day as monuments to the skill and accuracy of his surveying.

At the same time that the Turnpike surveys were being made, many of the Yorkshire rivers were being made navigable and their courses straightened and controlled.

A Yorkshireman, John Smeaton, of Austhorpe Hall, near Leeds, did much of this work, his first large job being the navigation of the Ure as far as Ripon, this stretch of navigable river being opened in 1770. An estimate of his for making the Aire navigable to Skipton includes the construction of locks and other features associated with the new canals which followed that date. The Duke of Bridgewater, with Brindley as his engineer, had planned and completed the first part of the canal from the coal mines at Worsley to Manchester, and then the manufacturers of the West Riding, largely under the inspiration of John Hustler and other Quakers of Bradford, planned the Leeds and Liverpool canal. The first portion of this, near Bingley, was opened in 1770, and the scheme was developed and completed across the Pennines early in the nineteenth century.

One of the canal schemes which was never carried out was that for a canal from Barnoldswick to Settle, in 1773. At the Settle end the important buildings round it were to be located in what is now called Chapel Fold. A very useful map of this survey was published on a scale of two inches to one mile.

The canals proved very successful and many schemes were proposed and lines surveyed. In this surveying the most essential feature was precise levelling and determination of heights. Up to this time, heights had been estimated in many ways, and some of the heights given to Yorkshire hills appear fantastic nowadays. Jefferys, of whose map we shall be speaking shortly, estimated Whernside as 5,340 feet; Ingleborough 5,280 feet; and Penyghent 5,220 feet, while Mr. Waddington made Pendle Hill 3,411 feet high!

The new methods of surveying introduced for the roads and canals, with the extension of methods of levelling, made it possible to produce maps which attempted to show the vertical height of the ground with some degree of accuracy, and which gave to hills their correct form, instead of including them on a map by purely pictorial and conventional signs.

We have wandered rather a long way from the actual maps of the county, but the background so gained will make the succeeding maps more intelligible. The first map to benefit to some extent by the advances in surveying was the great Yorkshire map by Jefferys, which we must now consider.

Thomas Jefferys was born in 1732 and died in 1771; he was the most prolific engraver and map publisher of the eighteenth century, and was appointed Geographer to the Prince of Wales and to George III. His first important publication was the engraved "Map of London," by William Morgan, in an edition prepared by Morden and Lea. The engraving of this map was very skilful and brought Jefferys an early reputation for good work. He joined with another map engraver, Thomas Kitchin, some of whose maps of Yorkshire we have already mentioned, and together they produced *The small English Atlas* in 1749.

Much of Jefferys' engraving was of a technical character for magazines and for the learned societies where extreme delicacy and accuracy were an essential, and this experience lies behind the beauty of the engraving of his map of Yorkshire. When Benjamin Donn made his survey of Devonshire and with it secured the first award of the Royal Society of Arts prize of £100, it was Jefferys who engraved the map for him, and who then got the idea of a similar map for Yorkshire. Between 1767 and 1770 he surveyed the county and completed his map only in the year of his death, so that it was published posthumously in 1772.

The map is on the scale of one inch to a mile, and is printed on twenty plates, each about 23 inches x 23 inches, the whole bound up in a large atlas. The sheets are divided into squares of five geographic miles wide, and these are numbered from west to east, 1 to 20 and lettered from north to south A to Q. Accompanying the atlas (but as loose sheets in the copy I possess) there are eleven sheets of a list or gazetteer of all the towns and hamlets on the map, with reference by number and letter to the square on which they occur, so that a quick reference to any place is very easily made. In addition to the one inch map, there is a key map to the county showing the area covered by each sheet, and also several engraved town plans: Ripon, Hull, Sheffield, Leeds, York and Scarborough. There are large views of Middleham Castle and Fountains Abbey, each occupying nearly a whole corner sheet which would have been empty if all the sheets had been mounted into one huge map.

For the first time on large-scale maps an attempt is made to represent the shape of the hills by hachuring—a series of finely-engraved lines, thick where the hill is steepest and thinning out as the slope lessens. The prominent hills and the valley slopes in the dales and in Cleveland are very strikingly shown, and with a high degree of accuracy. Many new features are included—he differentiates between turnpike roads and others—by heavier and very clear lining; shows lead and iron mines, alum pits, coal mines, windmills and water-mills. The projected line of the Leeds and Liverpool Canal is drawn on the map, and the Ripon Navigation running from Ripon to near Bishop Monkton, where it enters the river Ure by a lock. These are the only canals shown.

After his death the plates for the map were purchased by Robert Sayer, who re-printed from them in 1775. Other re-prints had been made in 1772 to 1775 by A. Dury, and on these, other projected canals are shown—one from Leeds to Selby, on a line which was never constructed; a final re-print was made by William Faden in 1800, an engraver closely associated with the early days of the Ordnance Survey.

After the issue of Jefferys' map there were many re-prints of smaller maps, but very little in the way of new work until the appearance in 1787 of maps by Cary. These were again small-scale atlas maps, but Cary was an engraver of very great skill and set new standards of clarity. His first maps were contained in his *New and Correct British Atlas: being a new set of County Maps from Actual Surveys . . .* This atlas is folio size and the maps are 9¾ inches by 7¾ inches and are usually lightly coloured. They show towns, villages, canals, roads with distances marked in figures alongside—rivers and bridges.

The rivers are shown, and hills are reduced to a light indication by hachured outlines, and are subdued to the rest of the information on the map. The survey of Yorkshire consisted of five sheets—a general outline map of the whole county which shows all the main roads with great prominence—but not much else. The North and East Ridings each have a complete sheet to themselves, and the West Riding occupies two sheets—a north part and a south part.

Two years later Cary engraved new maps of the county for the first edition of Gough's translation of Camden's *Britannia.* In this the maps were much larger, about 20 inches by 16 inches, and in their details were very similar to Jefferys' work. Cary also continued the tradition of Ogilby and Paterson by publishing in the same year his *Traveller's Companion, or a Deliniation of the Turnpike Roads of England and Wales . . . Laid down from the best authorities on a New Set of County Maps . . . etc.*

In 1798 Cary re-published the road guide in extended form, but without the county maps, under the title of: *Cary's New Itinerary, or an Accurate Deliniation of the Great Roads, both Direct and Cross, throughout England and Wales; with many of the Principal roads in Scotland, from an actual admeasurement made by Command of His Majesty's Postmaster General for Official Purposes; under the Direction and Inspection of Thomas Hasker, Esq., Surveyor and Superintendent of the Mail Coaches, by John Cary; Surveyor of the Roads to the General Post Office.*

In this task five surveyors were employed and an altogether new standard of accuracy was achieved. The volume has a small-scale map of England and Wales as frontispiece, showing all the post roads, and it is surprisingly clear when one considers the amount of information on it.

With this considerable experience, Cary became one of the most accurate of our map-makers, and his maps of Yorkshire were used and re-published in a total of forty-three editions before 1834, when the plates were bought by Cruchley, who from 1862 onwards re-titled them and issued them in several forms with railway and other additions in many subsequent years. Cary continued to do good service in map engraving, and his maps of the county, on a large scale, were used by William Smith for the first geological map—of which we shall have more to say in another chapter.

The Ordnance Survey

IN the last chapter we spoke of the work of John Cary, the map engraver who was already publishing maps before the end of the eighteenth century, and who continued his work well into the nineteenth. His largest and most important map of Yorkshire was produced in 1808, as *A New Map of Yorkshire . . .* showing roads, rivers and canals, and published in the *New English Atlas*. The map was in four sheets, 21 inches by 18 inches and was one of the very best so far published for the quality of the engraving. Cary's maps continued to be used for many purposes and we shall come across more examples in the next chapter. For the present we must leave them and give some time to the story and work of the Ordnance Survey.

It has been stated already that the difficulties experienced by the troops charged with the job of clearing up the rebels who had taken part in the second Jacobite Rebellion, 1745, had been greatly increased by the total lack of reliable maps of the Highlands of Scotland.

In 1747 the Deputy Quartermaster General, Lieutenant-General Watson, was very conscious of this and concerned about the lack of maps. He took it on himself to order a survey of the Highlands. A body of Infantry was posted to Fort Augustus, erected near the head of Loch Ness, Inverness-shire, and this fort was maintained until 1857.

Lord Blakeney was in command, and under him Watson and Assistant Quartermaster Roy began to make their map. This was a great undertaking, being actually a compass traverse with the detail filled in by field sketching, and mapped on a scale of a thousand yards to an inch. The sheets of this great survey are to be seen in the British Museum, King's Library, and were used as the basis for the reduced single-sheet map which was printed in 1774 in General Roy's *Military Antiquities of the Romans in North Britain.*

William Roy, born 1726 near Linlithgow, had joined the Army in 1747 from the Post Office at Edinburgh. In 1756 we come across him making reconnaissance surveys in England between Salisbury and Dorchester, and later in 1765, he was appointed to the new post of "Surveyor General of Coasts and Engineer for making and directing Military Surveys in Great Britain." His duties were laid down in detail and include, among others, "to inspect, survey and make reports from time to time of the Coasts and Districts of the Kingdom and the Islands theretobelonging." His pay was to be twenty shillings a day.

The years around 1783 became critical years for the birth of the survey; work was going on privately in many research directions, both here and in France, and in that year the French Ambassador at our Court presented the suggestion of a great French astronomer, M. Cassini de Thury, that astronomy would benefit if the observatories of Paris and Greenwich could be linked together by carefully surveyed lines and triangles to determine their precise positions. As the observatories were of foremost importance for navigation and time-keeping, this work was approved, and as Roy had already started for the benefit of his own work, the measurement of a base line near London, he was charged with the task of making a new base-line measurement on Hounslow Heath, from which it would be possible by triangulation to connect Greenwich with Dover, and make a link across the Channel to the French triangulation.

As triangulation is the basis of all the survey work, perhaps it would be well to state as simply as possible what is meant by the term. If a long straight line, of several miles, can be measured along the ground with extreme accuracy, and two other lines sighted by instruments, one from each end in directions which will make a triangle with the base line, and if the two end angles are measured with the same degree of accuracy, then the length of the two new sides can be calculated and the exact position of the apex of the triangle so made, is determined in this way.

A triangle on the opposite side of the base line will give another new point, and between the apexes of these two triangles a second base line is now known. Triangles can be made on the sides of the original ones, and this process goes on until the whole county can be covered by accurately measured triangles, the points of which can be calculated and laid down with certainty. Local detail within the triangles can then be measured from sides and points, and so the map is filled in. The points of the triangulation are prominent hill summits or church steeples, high towers, and so on, usually marked on the Ordnance map with a small triangle.

To measure a base line of about five miles length, with an accuracy sufficient for its extension to a national survey, new instruments had to be devised and made, and new scales engraved. Roy had a scale made of brass, 42 inches long and engraved in such a way that by the use of a vernier it could be read to one-thousandth of an inch. This scale had originally belonged to the early eighteenth-century Quaker instrument maker, Graham, and its finer dividing was done for Roy by a Mr. Bird. Other instruments, theodolites, were made for measuring the angles, and officers of the Engineers and Ordnance Corps were trained in their use.

The accuracy of observation and calculation attained was such that when a check base was measured on Romney Marsh, and then its length was calculated by triangulation from Hounslow Heath, the two lengths agreed to within 2.4ft. in a base length of 28,535.7 ft., or approximately an error of 1 in 12,000.

Later when the triangulation of the British Isles was completed, the calculation of the new base length on Salisbury Plain by triangulation made from the Irish base line, 350 miles distant, was only less than five inches different from the measurement, and again, the base line at Belhelvie was calculated from the Salisbury base, 422 miles away, through the vast network of intervening triangles, and was found to agree within a few inches of the measured length.

With a trained body of men and a measured base line, the time was ripe for an official survey and this was created by the Duke of Richmond in 1791. The Director was Lieutenant Colonel Edward Williams, assisted by Lieutenant Mudge and Isaac Dalby, and with a party of artillerymen to help in the fieldwork. The triangulation connecting England and France had been completed in 1787 and the connection from the Kent coast inland was in progress. The triangulation for this allowed the survey to begin the filling in of details for a one-inch to the mile map of Kent. At the same time Williams ordered the beginning of a map of the counties of Sussex and Essex.

The headquarters of the new Survey department were in the Tower, London, and their instruments were at first few in number, two one-hundred feet chains, a transit instrument for their astronomical observations, and a three-foot theodolite. The main object of the survey was the production of a one-inch to the mile map for the whole United Kingdom, and this remained their main work until 1824. The preparation of such a map demanded the completion of the major triangulation, and as this was to be the basis of all future surveys the highest possible degree of accuracy must be attained.

This was largely made possible by the skill of a Yorkshireman, Jesse Ramsden, the instrument maker, of Halifax birth. His father was a Halifax innkeeper and young Ramsden was brought up in the town until the time for his apprenticeship, when he went to London and was apprenticed with Burton, the mathematical instrument maker, in the Strand. This was in 1758 when he was twenty-three.

In 1765 when his apprenticeship was complete, he married the daughter of John Dolland, the great optician and optical instrument maker. Ramsden became one of the finest precision instrument makers of his time, and devised many improvements which made his work world famous. At one time he employed sixty workmen and still could not keep pace with his orders. He was a genius and like some other geniuses had no sense of time. It is told of him that on one occasion when he arrived at Buckingham House to see the King, in response to a Royal mandate, the King said to him that he was very punctual as to the hour and day—but late by a whole year!

Ramsden's greatest instrument was the 36 inch theodolite made for the King and presented by him to the Royal Society, and used in the first triangulation. This instrument was loaned to the survey by the Royal Society, and was in use from 1787 to 1853, a noble record.

One of the heavy tasks of the survey was to measure the length of an arc of meridian, from which to calculate all the necessary corrections in the preparation of their maps. The line chosen for this was 196 miles long, and stretched from Dunnose, near the southern extremity of the Isle of Wight, to Clifton, in Yorkshire, and for this measurement Ramsden made a new instrument, the zenith sector, with an 8 foot telescope and 4 inch object glass. For the triangulation needed, his theodolite was used, and for a check base measured on Misterton Carr, near Clifton, his two standard one-hundred foot chains did magnificent service. This base was 26,347.7 feet long. With these instruments and the data afforded by this measurement, the triangulation of England and Wales was completed in 1809, except for part of Lincoln, Norfolk, and Suffolk, and the work of making the map of the country could go on apace.

Returning now to the maps of Yorkshire, we come to another Yorkshireman who played an important part. Following the example of the Kent map, engraved by Faden, the first survey of Yorkshire was engraved by S. J. Neele & Sons, 352, Strand, London. This is known as Greenwood's map, and is titled, *Map of the County of York, Made on the Bases of Triangles in the County, determined by Lieut. Col. Wm. Mudge, Royal Artillery, F.R.S., and Capt. Thos. Colby, Royal Engrs. in the Trigonometrical Survey of England by Order of the Honourable Board of Ordnance, and surveyed in the years* 1815, 1816, *and* 1817, *by C. Greenwood, Wakefield. Engraved by S. J. Neele & Son, Published by the Proprietors, Robinson & Holdsworth, Leeds, John Hurst & C. Greenwood, Wakefield, June* 4*th*, 1817. . . . .

This is on a scale of Statute miles, 10 miles = 7¼ inches. It is in nine sheets, 27½ inches x 23 inches, and was issued with the sheets stitched together in a rough atlas. The whole were re-issued in 1828 by Teesdale, as Teesdale's *Atlas of Yorkshire*.

The county maps by Jefferys, of which we have already discussed the one of Yorkshire, were, many of them, hachured —that is, hill-shaded. This hachuring was still somewhat experimental and crude, and tended on the Yorkshire map to make the Dales look like very steep-sided trenches cut into a nearly level plateau. The officers and draughtsmen of the Ordnance Survey experimented with hachuring and soon developed a new technique so that the hachures really showed the shape of the ground with considerable accuracy. This new hachuring was used by Faden in his map of Kent. Faden was Geographer to His Majesty the King and to His Royal Highness the Prince Regent, and as he was only employed by the survey to engrave their maps, he was able to carry on his own business at the same time. Among many county maps he published, there is in 1816, A *Map of the County of York, Reduced from the large Survey in Twenty Sheets of the late Thomas Jefferys, and Drawn from a scale of two Statute Miles to One Inch. Revised and Corrected to the present Time.* This was in four sheets each $27\frac{1}{2}$ inches by $22\frac{3}{4}$ inches, and is our first "half-inch" map. The engraving is excellent and the map used the 1800 edition of Jefferys which is the most accurate. There are a few minor corrections to the line of the Huddersfield-Rochdale Canal and to the heights of the mountains, while a few new roads are added—e.g., the Addingham-Draughton-Skipton new road.

The Ordnance Survey one-inch to one mile survey of Britain progressed slowly during the next thirty years, but for the next advance in survey practice we must look to Ireland. A Committee on the Survey and Valuation of Ireland had reported to Parliament in June, 1824, and pointed out that because land measures varied and there were no accurately mapped boundaries of townships, parishes, and fields, their assessments were bound to be inadequate. After considering many recommendations, Parliament voted the sum of £5,000 towards the cost of a trigonometrical survey of Ireland, and the Committee concerned strongly suggested that this should be on a scale of six-inches to the mile, as the least scale on which areas could be accurately shown. The scale was adopted, and as a preliminary to the survey a base line was measured along the eastern shore of Lough Foyle. The whole of Ireland was covered on the six-inch scale and the mapping was completed in 1846.

In the meantime, Scotland had asserted herself, on the ground that the triangulation, in Scotland had been stopped in 1825 and nothing was available but the first rough military survey. Many individuals and the corporations of many of her towns and cities memorialised Parliament for a complete survey and, as a result, in 1837 Parliament authorised the survey of Scotland and the six northern counties of England on the six-inch to the mile basis. This work was started, but many new problems were raised which need mention here in connection with our Yorkshire map.

In the course of the triangulation, the angles from various positions to the summits of mountains had been measured, including both the horizontal and the vertical angles, and from these records the heights of about three hundred hills had been calculated, A Committee of the British Association for the Advancement of Science investigated the measurement of heights and concluded that precise levelling from sea level was the more accurate method, and in 1839 the Irish Survey adopted this. There was, of course, the question of finding a suitable datum to which all heights could be referred, and for this the level of the low water of a spring tide, at Poolbeg Lighthouse, Dublin Bay, on 8th April, 1837, was used.

When the English branch of the Survey began the levelling of England and Wales in 1840, a different datum was used, that of mean sea level at Liverpool, determined by taking the level of the tide at Victoria Dock every five minutes for about an hour around high and low water, every tide from the 7th to the 16th of March. This old datum served until well into this century when the new one was determined as the mean sea level at Newlyn, Cornwall. This was calculated from the hourly readings of an automatic tide gauge reading from 1st of May, 1915, to 30th of April, 1921, and is the O.D. (Ordnance Datum) to which all heights on the maps are now referred. The Irish heights are about 8 feet more than this as they refer to low water.

With the accurate determination of heights and the precise levelling across country of the new survey, a demand arose for the representation of continuous height on a map. Railways and canals wanted accurate levels, and the growth of towns created problems of drainage and water supply which demanded maps with numerous levels upon them. Again several committees considered the matter and as the result of many representations the Survey in 1844 adopted the use of contour lines. Yorkshire is fortunate in having its six-inch to the mile maps contoured at 25 feet intervals a feature shared by Lancashire and the northern counties, but the later six-inch mapping of the rest of the country generally had contours only at 100 feet intervals. Fortunately for us, the one-inch maps of the county were produced at the very peak of hachuring skill, and the six-inch maps at the time when close contouring was practised. Thus we get the best of both worlds and have maps which are an artistic delight as well as an accurate delineation of the country.

The description of these maps and the other scale maps which were introduced at various times, will have to wait for a later section. It is sufficient to say here that the Ordnance Survey of Yorkshire on the six-inch scale was completed between 1845 and 1854 in 311 sheets each 36 inch by 24 inch with contours at 25 feet intervals up to 1,200 feet O.D., then at 50 feet intervals above that. This survey included all authentic archaeology, historic sites, natural features, walls, plantations, etc., and is the fullest and finest map ever issued.

Geological and Enclosure Maps

THE story of the Ordnance Survey up to the first publication of the six-inch to the mile maps of Yorkshire brings us to the year 1850, and we shall need now to fill in some other detail about the maps published during the first half of the century. Our first note must be about the geological map, by which the area of ground occupied by each different kind of rock is shown by some significant colour. This type of map was first put forward in a practical form by Dr. Martin Lister, a Yorkshire physician, as early as 1684. Martin Lister was the son of Sir Martin Lister, and was educated at St. John's College, Cambridge. He became a fellow of his college in 1660 and soon developed a profound knowledge of zoology. In 1670 he was elected a Fellow of the Royal Society, and settled in York as a physician. His correspondence with the eminent naturalist, John Ray, and with other learned people covers very wide interests, and includes letters on the plants and spiders of Craven; he was the first person to study spiders scientifically. He was equally interested in antiquities and sent many Roman remains to the Ashmolean Museum, Oxford. In 1684 he removed to London, and in the next few years completed his great work on the *History of Shells.* In 1709 he became Second Physician in Ordinary to Queen Anne, but died three years after his appointment.

His suggestions for a geological map occur in a letter sent to the Royal Society, entitled: *An Ingenious proposal for a new sort of Maps of Countrys, together with tables of Sands and Clays such as are chiefly found in the North of England.* In this he says that different rocks can be shown by colours or shading.

"But the great care must be very exactly to note on the map where such and such soils are bounded. As for example in

Yorkshire. 1. The Woolds: chaulk, flint and pyrites, etc. . . 4. Western Mountains: moores, sandstone, coal, ironstones, lead-ore, sand, clay, etc. . . . Now if it were noted how far these extended, and the limits of each soil appeared upon a map, something more might be comprehended from the whole or from every part than I can possibly foresee, which would make such a labour well worth the pains."

This suggestion was based upon the observations made by him while collecting material for his various works, and his field studies convinced him that there was a definite and recognisable order in the occurrence of rock strata, and that the rocks were by no means just scattered in chaos.

Another Yorkshireman, the Rev. John Michell, Rector of Thornley, near Wakefield, and an intimate friend of Smeaton, the Leeds engineer, followed on the work of Martin Lister, and was soon convinced that in the Pennines there was an orderly succession of rock layers, and that the long rocky scarps that make so much of the Pennine scenery belonged to the outcropping edges of layers of rock that could be seen to have a regular order. He recognised that the layers of rock on each side of the Pennines were similar and were newer than those in the centre, and so saw for the first time the elementary structure of these hills.

Much of his time was spent in the country and he soon acquired a very competent knowledge of the rocks, both of West and of East Yorkshire. He also felt that the facts he had learned could best be recorded by sections of strata or some form of map. He made a most important communication to the Royal Society in 1760 in a paper on *Conjectures concerning the Cause and Observations upon the Phenomena of Earthquakes,* in which he gives a most lucid description of the structure of the North of England.

Some examples of the work of John Smeaton of Austhorpe, near Leeds, are known to everyone, and none better than his construction of the Eddystone Lighthouse, but it is not often appreciated that Smeaton was in some ways an accomplished geologist. In his design for the Eddystone Lighthouse he needed a particular kind of lime which would set and not deteriorate in the presence of sea water, and he found such a lime in the lias strata of Glamorganshire. He studied the strata in which this occurred, and then by actual mapping, traced the same bed across country as far as Newark-on-Trent, thus anticipating some of the work of William Smith.

To mention all who contributed to this early development of geology would be tedious, but it would include a large number of Yorkshiremen; some mention, however, must be given to the work of the agricultural surveys of 1794 and the following years, published for each county by the Board of Agriculture. Many of the volumes include a map which is coloured to show the different soils. The Yorkshire survey was published in 1794, and there are two maps—one of the East Riding and one of the North Riding—by Isaac Leatham and John Tuke, respectively, which are very cleanly coloured to show soils.

We must, however, pass on to the work of William Smith, "the father of English geology," who made the first large-scale geological maps, by a detailed survey of the ground. In 1799 he had published a map of the country five miles round Bath, and in 1801 a *General Map of the strata found in England and Wales*. In 1815 he completed a large-scale map of England and Wales, five miles to the inch, coloured geologically, and employing twenty different colours. This was followed by county maps, that of Yorkshire being published in 1821 on an impression of Cary's county map of 1818. It is said to be one of the finest and when compared with the official maps of H.M. Geological Survey it is seen to be of a high order of accuracy.

To revert to the Ordnance Survey, its Director, Colonel Mudge, had a letter in 1814 from Colonel Chapman asking if a mineralogical and geological surveyor could be attached to the Survey. Dr. McCulloch, who had already done much work on the geology of Scotland, was suggested, as the geologist was primarily needed in order to point out and determine places where the geology was such that large deflections of the plumb-line from true vertical might be expected. In 1826 McCulloch started a geological map of Scotland, completing it in 1834 on Arrowsmith's map, but complaining of the inaccuracy of this map for his work. A committee of geologists, Adam Sedgwick of Dent, Buckland, and Lyell, urged that a geological survey should be founded to undertake the preparation of geological surveys and the publication of maps, and this suggestion was accepted and the Geological Survey was started in 1835 under Sir Henry De la Beche who was at that time engaged on the geology of Cornwall and Devon, and these counties were the first to be completed.

In Yorkshire the Geological Survey was soon at work and its officers were stimulated by the Yorkshire Geological

Society, founded in 1837. The first survey of the geology was traced upon the hachured one-inch to the mile editions of the Ordnance Survey maps, and coloured in by hand. In many areas of the Dales these maps were until recently the only edition available, but now much progress is being made in a re-survey. These revised maps are being issued in a colour printed edition.

The first sheets of the geological survey for Yorkshire were those around Sheffield, published in 1852. These surveys were largely the work of John Phillips, the nephew of William Smith, and for long connected with the Yorkshire Philosophical Society at York. He was joined by A. H. Green who eventually produced the monumental memoir on the Geology of the Yorkshire Coalfield, and by J. R. Dakyns, who became more specifically connected with the survey of the Dales area from Clitheroe northward to Crossfell. Dakyns was joined by R. H. Tiddeman in most of the Dales' mapping, and Tiddeman for much of the time lived in or was associated with Skipton, and his big collection of fossils is now in the Craven Museum.

A large general map of the geology of Yorkshire was prepared and printed by John Phillips in 1853, and remained a very useful index map until the publication of the four miles to one inch map by the Geological Survey, in five sheets, between 1889 and 1907. The mapping for the geological surveys was carried out on the six-inch to the mile sheets, and after reduction onto the one-inch maps, the six-inch mapping was transferred to six-inch sheets for printing, and these were issued for the county in three hundred large sheets, 36 inches by 24 inches, between 1868 and 1882. Memoirs were prepared to accompany the one-inch sheets, and most but not all of these were published, describing the details of the geology for the strict area depicted on the sheet.

During the latter half of the nineteenth century, with the maps of the Ordnance Survey available, there was a new standard of accuracy; smaller and special maps, which appeared in large numbers, tended more and more to be reduced from the official survey maps. There were the maps now included in directories, maps of railways, canals, roads, maps to accompany the Census Report, for commissions on Local Government boundaries, and for a hundred and one different purposes, and it would be impossible in this short book to do anything more than provide a very dull and incomplete catalogue. We can therefore turn for relief to another kind of map and surveyor which was produced in the latter part of the eighteenth and early nineteenth centuries—that associated with the Enclosure Awards and the Tithe Awards.

The Enclosure Acts, by which the remnants of the old common fields were enclosed and awarded to a limited number of owners, were only made possible on the basis of very accurate surveys, and in the throng of the Enclosure movement many local surveyors were trained and became in great demand for their skill in surveying and map-drawing. Each Enclosure Act specifies, usually in a very similar clause, that a careful map shall be made, sometimes naming the surveyor. An example will show the procedure. In the Act authorising the enclosure of common fields in Appletreewick, 1815, section VII reads:

"And be it further enacted, That for more just and regular Division of the said Lands and Grounds hereby directed to be divided, allotted and enclosed, a perfect Survey and Admeasurement and Map thereof shall be made by Samuel Swire the younger of Halifax, in the said County of York, Land Surveyor, and in the case of his Death, Neglect, Inability, or Refusal to act, then by such other fit, competent, and impartial Person, as the said Commissioners shall appoint; and such Survey and Admeasurement shall be reduced into Writing, and the Number of Acres, Roads, and Perches in the said stinted Pastures, Open Field Lands, Moor or Common, be therein set forth and ascertained; and such Survey and Admeasurement and Map shall be laid before the said Commissioners, to be used by them for the Purposes of this Act; and the said Surveyor and the said Commissioners, their Assistants and Servants respectively, shall have full Power and Authority at any Time, until the said intended Inclosure be completed, and the Award of the said Commissioners duly signed and perfected, to enter upon view, examine, and admeasure the said Lands and Grounds hereby directed to be divided and inclosed."

The surveyor was then bound by an oath which was to be administered by "the said Commissioners, or either of them, to administer to each and every Surveyor as aforesaid; and such Oath, so taken and subscribed, shall be enrolled, annexed to, and deposited with the award of the said Commissioners. The wording of this section is hardly changed from the similar ones in the identical wording, for other Awards, apart from the naming of the surveyor.

When the surveyor had completed his work he prepared his

map, of which a copy was usually drawn on parchment, and then, in the earlier awards, attached to the roll of the award. Later it became the custom to prepare a large copy of the map, which in many cases was lodged in the parish church. The maps are of great interest as they include the names by which all the fields were known at the time of the inclosure, and it is usually possible to reconstruct the old common fields from them. The name of an ancient field will spread over several new inclosures, and may be differentiated by such additions as Near Barnscar, Far Barnscar, and so on, or the addition of the new owner's name—e.g., Proctor High Mark, Atkinson High Mark, Sergeantson High Mark, etc., all of which are inclosed parts of one old common. Much of our local history is buried in these maps, as well as much other information of current value.

The inclosure Commissioners had the power to stop up or divert footpaths and bridle-ways, and to apportion land for roads in place of the old tracks that just wandered over the driest bits of the commons. The maps show the allotted footpaths and roads, and though these are never all the footpaths that existed, still their appearance on the inclosure award places them beyond any question as right of way. The map also marks the walls, and shows which part of them, for building and repair, belongs to which piece of land. Turf allotments, "poor's Grass," charity lands of various kinds, the township quarry where freeholders can get stone for repair of houses, etc., are often marked, and the map is a reference document that is essential for the settling of many vexed disputes even at present.

The quality of the work of these old surveyors is very high, their work being of the very finest, both in quality of line, beauty of lettering, and general layout. Some, of course, are not so good, but on the whole the maps are a delight to see and to study. The inclusion of the exact acreage of all inclosures was important for tithe purposes as well as for taxation, sale, etc., and there was some agitation throughout the country for a national map on which acreage could be recorded, so that such a record would be valid for appeal in cases of sale, conveyance or dispute about land. This was met eventually by the cadastral survey, on the scale of one two-thousand-five-hundredth, or 25.344 inches to the mile, the scale usually called the twenty five inch. On this scale of the Ordnance Survey maps, each inclosure, large or small, is numbered, and the area stated, and the number and the area are acceptable reference for any purpose.

This large-scale map has no contours, but along the roads has the "spot heights" of the main levelling, and bench marks are shown. These are the familiar Government broad arrow, with a line over the top carved on rock faces, gate-posts, or the corner-stones of buildings, anywhere that seems reasonably permanent and immovable. The bench mark is carefully levelled to the centre of the top line, and the level is marked on the 25 inch map to the nearest tenth of a foot, appearing on the map as "B.M. 680.7" for example.

In many parishes there is still, carefully preserved, the Tithe Award map, which is usually a large-scale survey of all the fields in the parish, with the names of owners at the time of the survey, and an accompanying schedule of the fields and the tithe due from them. These maps often have more detail even than the inclosure map, and are the final appeal for field names and field studies. The Tithe maps were most of them made around 1836 to 1840 and are very useful for historic reference.

The variety of private surveys being made of gentlemen's estates, of mining properties and of railway routes, was probably at a maximum just before the appearance of the 25 inch maps, but for our county of Yorkshire alone, they would run into many thousands, the work of many hundreds of different surveyors, so that it would be impossible to do more than give a very partial and inadequate account of a few examples, unless at some time, the different surveys for a single parish could be collected, and used as typical of the wider area, and that lies outside the scope of this book.

Making the Most of Maps

MOST map-lovers have a collection, large or small, of rather shabby old maps, mostly one-inch or half-inch to a mile, weather stained and going at the seams, and these form a library of happy associations. Hours can be spent over any one of them, recalling happy days on the fells or in the lowlands. Pleasant incidents attach to most of the place-names. The maps have been friends and guides on countless journeys and will be on many more. Such maps have shown the way, told us the names of places, taught us the lie of the land and led us in kindly and encouraging manner to learn the land and its features in a way hardly possible otherwise. A good map is a companion-guide and teacher, and a friendly possession.

During the years of this century a new function of the map has gradually emerged, that of the instrument of research and discovery, and now almost any serious investigation involving history, archaeology, or any of the natural sciences, will invoke the aid of the map, both for the discovery of new facts and for their display. The basis of much of this new use of maps is the method of recording on them the distribution of some one or other selected phenomena or occurences, seeing if these fall into any distinct areas or patterns, then comparing the distributions with such features as topography, the geology, rainfall, soil and so on. From the relations so obtained it is often found that a new fact will emerge throwing light on past events which probably could be arrived at in no other way. At the same time the distributions in space demonstrated by plotting on a map will often bring to light questions and problems that can lead to further profitable research. In all modern town and country planning, maps are becoming one of the basic tools of the planner, and without them many of his ideas could hardly be presented in an intelligible form, except perhaps to the expert. After all, the map is a two dimensional representation of a country side or of an assemblage of facts, vastly more factual and detailed than any other form of picture.

A good example of this newer use of maps as a research tool can be seen in the recent study of place-names as a clue to early history. On a map of Yorkshire, say a quarter inch to a mile, put a different coloured ring round village and town names with different groups of endings. Use one colour for all the names which end in *-by*, like Earby, Wetherby and so on; use another colour for *-ton*, and *-ley*, Flockton say, and Beverley; still another colour for names ending in *-gill*, like Masongill, though most of these names will be of isolated farm houses. We could include in the *-gill* names those which are used for stream valleys, Sleets Gill, Easegill, and so on to a very great number. It would be convenient (speaking from later knowledge) to include hamlets and farms which terminate in *-sett*, Burtersett, Appersett, and others.

If this is done carefully for a large area, and particularly if your area crosses the Pennines, say from North Lancashire to the Cleveland Hills, you will soon see a distinct pattern appearing. The *-gill* and *-sett* names will lie dominantly in the north-west and in the higher fell country; *-ley* and *-ton* names will fill the valleys and the plain towards the east, and the *-by* names will tend to cling together down the west side of the vale of York and in some other areas around the valley mouths.

Now what does this pattern mean? These three different groups of names were given by three different groups of people who settled in Yorkshire before the Norman Conquest, Danes, Angles and Norsemen. You will see that the Norse names are thicker towards the west and north-west, thinning out and becoming rare to the east, while the opposite is true of the Danish names. We know now that the Norse invaded our country from the west, coming round the north of Scotland and down the west coast to north Ireland and the Isle of Man then across on to our hills, while the Angles came via the east coast and then up the eastward flowing rivers. Norsemen liked the hilltop pasture and Angles preferred the fertile land of the valley bottoms. Danes came as raiders, penetrated to areas they liked and tended to cluster near together rather than to spread over the whole land.

This picture presented here in scantiest detail (see *Vikings, Angles and Danes,* a *Dalesman* booklet, for a fuller story) is the foundation of our knowledge of how these people came and which areas they claimed and settled, and the map-pattern of place-names has filled in a period of our history for which we have only the briefest written records. A carefully prepared map of this distributional kind, is capable of presenting a striking picture which carries conviction in every line and dot.

Special distribution maps of an enormous number of facts and factors have now appeared in technical literature, and the number of publications using distribution maps is increasing every day. A very interesting stimulus was given to this kind of work by one of our Yorkshire field naturalists, Dr. T. W. Woodhead, of the Tolson Memorial Museum, Huddersfield. All through the 1920s Dr. Woodhead was editing and publishing the museum handbooks written by himself and other experts, describing Huddersfield in prehistoric, Roman, and other periods. In 1931 he prepared, himself, a handbook of outstanding importance, *Climate, Vegetation and Man in the Huddersfield District.* This contains fourteen maps which display the geology, rainfall, vegetation and topography, and then the distribution of man. The vegetation is shown for many of the recognised prehistoric periods and from the Ice Age up to 1900. The accompanying text demonstrates the intimate relation of man and the history of the area to its climate and vegetation through all that long time. It is a masterpiece of distribution mapping.

The Ordnance Survey from 1924 has published distribution maps for Britain, which cover many periods—Iron Age, Roman, Anglo-Saxon, Mediaeval and even Seventeenth Century. This last map includes the roads which were mapped by Ogilby in his survey of 1675. The maps are all accompanied by an authoritative but brief text, and they represent one of the finest of the recent series of maps.

At the present time there is a rapid spread of the study of Local History, or in schools often the wider based Local Studies, which include geography, geology and the biological studies. In these fields of interest the older maps are ceasing to be merely fashionable wall ornaments and are becoming the tools of research. The town plans on Speed's maps are an invaluable point in the history of a town; the position of bridges, the post towns indicated on the earlier maps, the road system before the Turnpikes, all are of interest and provide a mass of evidence for a local study. The first edition of the Ordnance Survey maps, both one inch and six inch present an unsurpassed picture of the towns and countryside of more than a hundred years ago. No maps have been more finely prepared than some of the sheets of that first edition, and no one who loves maps can afford not to visit his library and to ponder over these maps of any area in which he has a special interest.

Every map-user ought to have at least the six inch maps of his own immediate district, and they ought to fill up slowly with manuscript notes and additions until in time a second and third copy is needed to accommodate one's observations. Field names, boundary marks, quarries, natural history jottings, all can find a place on the six inch map, even if only a tiny reference number can find room, so long as a good note book or index of references is also kept. An old and well-used six inch map is in itself a note book of local observation and history. The work of map recording never ends and it is an occupation always stirred by the possibility of new discovery and by the thrill of adding a little more to one's knowledge of the countryside or the town in which one lives or seeks recreation in leisure hours.